EXPLORING

BIBLE GUIDE TO
JOHN'S GOSPEL

EXPLORING GOD'S WORD

BIBLE GUIDE TO JOHN'S GOSPEL

Donald Guthrie

HODDER AND STOUGHTON
LONDON   SYDNEY   AUCKLAND   TORONTO

British Library Cataloguing in Publication Data

Guthrie, Donald
    Exploring God's word: Bible guide
to John's Gospel. – (Hodder Christian
paperbacks)
    1. Bible. N. T. John – Commentaries
    I. Title
226′.507   BS2615.3

    ISBN 0-340-39942-4

Contents

5

6

Chapter 8

Chapter 9

Chapter 10

Chapter 11

Chapter 12

Chapter 13

Chapter 19

Chapter 20

Chapter 21

Preface

The reader might be interested to know what prompted the writing of this series of Bible Guides. It arose from a desire to promote more expositional study of the biblical text.

I had frequently had recourse to the Pulpit Commentary for suggestions for homiletical structures, but recognised the need for something more concise and relevant. The present series presents a collection of outlines on which it is hoped that the reader will be able to build. Only those outlines which arise naturally out of the text itself have been included.

I am grateful to the publishers who at every stage have encouraged me in the conception and working out of the project.

General Introduction

The purpose of these guides is to provide a tool for the expositional study of the biblical text. There are many different approaches to the study of Scripture, but our aim will be to begin with the scriptural text with the purpose of discovering what contribution it can make to the life of the Christian.

Each guide will consist of a number of outlines which are designed to assist the Bible student to gain an orderly understanding of the content and meaning of the text. It is hoped that this will provide an exciting field of study. Although the aim is exegetical, that is, to discover what the text actually says, the need to see how the text can be personally applied to daily life has been a major factor in the production of the outlines.

In personal study, in group study and for homiletical purposes there is no substitute for the orderly presentation of the Scriptures.

Each biblical book is split into sections. For each selection of verses, different outlines are provided, one or two for the whole section and others for smaller parts. These are arranged in order according to the starting verse of each section. A glance at the table of contents will clearly demonstrate this arrangement.

Some overlapping within the outlines is unavoidable, but the various combinations illustrate the different approaches that can be made to the text.

It is hoped that the outlines provided will serve as a catalyst for the development of other outlines.

THE GOSPEL OF JOHN
Introduction

About the purpose of the gospel

We are fortunate that the evangelist thought to tell us
precisely why he wrote his gospel. He sets out his purpose
in chapter 20:30, 31. His target was to lead his readers to a
particular kind of faith in Jesus. He was not setting out the
story of a mere man. His gospel was about the Christ, the
Son of God. This was a particular way of looking at Jesus.
Faith in such a way would lead to life, spiritual life. The
purpose was therefore in the truest sense evangelistic. The
evangelist wanted people to be influenced by what he
wrote.

Because the book begins as it does, making use of some
special terminology which was in use among Greek speaking people, we may deduce that the writer wanted to make
Jesus known to a fairly wide audience, although his use of
the title Christ (Messiah) shows he had Jews very much in
his mind.

About the structure of the gospel

When compared with the other gospels, John stands apart
from them in that in this gospel the events happen mainly in
Jerusalem instead of Galilee. This accounts for the difference of structure. From 1:19 to the end of chapter 12 the
material is arranged around a series of signs. This is followed by a section which has sometimes been known as the
farewell section (13–17) and which leads into the passion
narrative. The latter runs more closely parallel to the other
gospels although it has its unique features. The whole is
introduced by what may be called a prologue (1:1–18) and
concludes with what may be called an epilogue (Jn. 21).

About the date of the gospel

It is difficult to date the gospel with any degree of accuracy. But there are indications that a date within the lifetime of the apostles is most probable. The author himself claims to have been an eyewitness and this must limit the possibilities for fixing the date. The evidence from the early Christian period points to the fact that this book was received as authoritative at least in the second century and this supports a date much earlier in the first century. It has been suggested that the book may have been written before the fall of Jerusalem (AD 70), and there is no compelling reason for supposing it is later. It cannot be later than the last decade of the first century, since a few verses of the gospel have been preserved in the John Rylands fragment which was found in Egypt and dates from early in the second century.

About the author of the gospel

The author does not introduce himself. We are therefore largely dependent on early church reports and there is no doubt from these that the book was at an early stage believed to be the work of John the apostle. Such a strong tradition is supported by the indications of an eyewitness account, by the author's evident knowledge of Palestine and of Jewish affairs.

The fact that a gospel so different from the others was accepted within the Christian church requires at least an author of some influence to explain it. While we cannot prove the tradition, there are no overriding considerations which would exclude it. That the writer is familiar with Greek thought has seemed to some sufficient to rule out a Galilean fisherman as the writer. But since our knowledge of this particular Galilean fisherman's grasp of Greek thought is nil, it is precarious to base any conclusion on it. Nevertheless some prefer to regard the author as a member of a Johannine school or to regard him as a rather shadowy John the elder. Our conclusions over who wrote the gospel will affect our interpretation of the writing only if those conclusions undermine its authoritative character.

JOHN 1:1–18
Introducing
Jesus Christ

*John begins with a prologue which provides
many signposts to themes found in the gospel.
It points to a wonderful person.*

A preview of his character (1–5)
(a) *He was God.* This is dramatically stated in terms of the
Word who was with God. This statement cannot be
fathomed.
(b) *He was the giver of life.* He created everything and gave
life to the human race. He is seen as the sole agent of
creation.
(c) *He was the light that dispelled the darkness.* That light
has never gone out.
What he was he still is.

An announcement of his coming (6–8)
John the Baptist is seen as a necessary witness. It was all
part of the divine plan. He pointed beyond himself. The
main purpose was to get people to believe in Christ.

A declaration of his purpose (9–13)
(a) *He came to affect everyone.* He brought illumination.
Only through him can people know God.
(b) *He came to an adverse world.* The world did not know
him. His own people did not receive him.
(c) *He enables believers to become sons.* This is brought
about, not by natural means, but by God's will.

17

A revelation of his glory (14–18)

(a) *Through incarnation.* The Word dwelt among us so
that we could see his glory. John speaks as an eyewitness. It was a glory from the Father through the
Son. This was a tremendous mystery.

(b) *Through the testimony of another.* John the Baptist
recognised Christ's superiority to himself.

(c) *Through a better way than through law.* Moses experienced God's glory – but nothing compared with Christ.
No one ever saw God except the Son – who better to
make him known!

(d) *Through his incomparable gifts.* Grace and truth came
through Christ. The whole Gospel amply illustrates
this.

> *The prologue provides such rich insights
> that should whet our appetites to read on.
> At the same time we could linger for long
> over it without ever losing our wonder at
> what God has done.*

JOHN 1:1, 14
The Word

> *This seems a strange way to begin a
> gospel. But we are at once plunged into
> deep thinking. John takes up a Greek idea
> pointing to thought and speech. He invites
> us to consider the Word and then identifies
> him as Jesus.*

The eternity of the Word

'In the beginning'

Origins have a fascination for us. But how do we cope with
the 'beginning of all things'? John intends to make us think
of the time before anything existed.

The Word was already there. He is seen as greater than
all things, greater than time, changeless as eternity.

The environment of the Word

'The word was with God'

The problem here is to think back before creation. We are invited to think about the environment of the Word. Unlike man's environment, the Word's was perfect.

There is mystery here. The Word is separate from God. There was perfect fellowship between God and the Word.

The essence of the Word

'The word was God'

This reaches the peak of the mystery. John introduces the deity of Christ before his humanity. Many modern movements approach it in the reverse order.

This statement means that if we know the Word we know God, and if we know God we know the Word. We could not be confronted with profounder thoughts at the beginning of an account of Jesus Christ.

The expression of the Word

'The Word became flesh'

Against the background of such profound thoughts, we are at length presented with a man. Why did the Word become flesh?

It was to make God known. It was to provide a way for men to become sons of God. It was to bring to men grace and truth. None of these things could have happened apart from the Word taking on a human form.

After such an introduction no one should rush into the gospel without profound respect. John is to relate no ordinary life, but an account of perfect God who became perfect man. He wants us to know this from the beginning. The gospel begins with a mystery which makes us want to discover more.

JOHN 1:5
Light and darkness

*The world is full of contrasts. John uses the
natural contrast between light and darkness to
enhance the splendour of the light, whom he
identifies as Christ. Later he tells us Christ
called himself the light (8:12).*

The shining light

Although not yet named, it is clear Christ is meant.

(a) *It is essential for life.* The rays of the sun are necessary to life. A world without Christ is spiritually dead.
The light brings life and health.

(b) *It stands for purity.* The sun shining in a dark room
shows up every speck of dust. Works of evil prefer
the darkness, but Christ dwells in perfect light,
where holiness flourishes.

(c) *It symbolises knowledge.* Man's mind has been en-
lightened through Christ. He brought understanding
and true knowledge.

(d) *It gives guidance.* How valuable is a light on a dark
night to discover the way! But when the Light is a
person, it is much superior. The light becomes a
personal guide.

(e) *It is linked with glory.* Think of the sheer beauty of
the setting sun on banks of clouds in summer. Glory
can best be described in terms of light (cf. Heb. 1:3).
But even light is a pale figure to describe the glory of
God in Christ.

(f) *It is unique.* Christ is not *a* light, but *the* light. There
may be others who bring some illumination but their
light is at best derived. The New Testament portrays
Christ as unique.

The contrasting darkness

(a) *An appropriate figure for a fallen world.* Darkness
symbolises ignorance. Jesus called the religious
leaders blind. In spite of his high intelligence, man is

basically spiritually blind (cf. 2 Cor. 4:4). Resort to violence is an extreme example of this.

(b) *Darkness typifies sin*. Most evil deeds are done away from the glare of publicity. Sin thrives in ignorance and spiritual deadness. When the Light shone, it brought man's darkness into stark focus.

The relation between light and darkness.

The text here is ambiguous.

(a) *Darkness could not overcome it*. Evil in the form of darkness has often tried to extinguish the light of the gospel. Apathy, decadence, materialism have encroached on the light. But darkness has never succeeded.

(b) *Darkness could not comprehend it*. An alternative understanding of the word. The gospel was not overcome, but neither was it understood by the majority. When the most brilliant Light shone most people were unaware of it.

The most relevant question to face is whether the Light has shone in our darkness.

JOHN 1:10, 11
The light the world never saw

Jesus came into a world of strife, moral decadence, ignorance, multifarious religious cults, tyranny. Our modern world differs little. What John observed in his day has an ongoing relevance.

The Coming of Light

In creation God said, Let light be.

In the incarnation, Light appeared in human form.

In both cases there was power to shatter darkness, the one physical, the other spiritual.

(a) *God was becoming man*. It had never happened

before. It was a unique event. That is why it continues to perplex. Some deny that Jesus was God and think the mystery disappears. But John has made it clear that the Light was God.

(b) *The Coming was an act of condescension*. Why did perfect Light single out this speck of a world in the greatness of the universe? Here is mystery – but the purpose was to save the people of this world.

(c) *The Coming was an act of illumination*. John sees Christ as the illuminator of men. This is not the only result of the coming, but it is suggestive. True knowledge is seen to come from only one source.

The Creative Power of the Light

John repeats this idea from verse 5. It is clearly important for his theme.

(a) *It shows the right of Jesus to come into the world*. He became a creature in the very world he had created. It was a voluntary act on his part.

(b) *It explains his deep concern for mankind*. God is no disinterested inventor. He continues to watch over his creation. That is why Jesus came.

The plan of salvation is a continuation of the act of creation.

The Rejection of the Light

The statement that the world knew him not is tragic. How could man miss such a glorious Light? This is one of history's great enigmas.

(a) *The world must bear responsibility*. He was there in closest proximity. The rejection amounted to a deliberate refusal.

(b) *The world suffered the greatest possible loss as a consequence*. It doomed itself to a continuation of groping. It is incredible that the world still rejects.

Whether men acknowledge the fact or not, the Light has shone. It constantly challenges us. How foolish it is to draw down the blinds to shut it out!

JOHN 1:14
The incarnation

John's opening tells more about the significance of Jesus' coming than the other Gospels. It provides a kind of pre-history. It is not easy reading, but will stretch the mind that reflects on it.

It shows the pre-existence of Christ

Jesus was no ordinary man. His cause was no mere experiment. It was planned.

But why did John begin like this? To let us know at once the background of the coming of Christ. It was God breaking into history.

It shows the true humanity of Jesus

Since he became 'flesh', he became the same sort of person as we are – with our feelings and limitations (though without sin).

But why did he do this? The kernel of the gospel is that he identified himself with us in all our need.

It shows the temporary character of Christ's earthly life

The word 'dwelt' is drawn from the tabernacle in the wilderness. God never intended him to be permanently on earth. The death of Christ was part of the plan – the human life was a temporary necessity.

It shows that the coming was fully authenticated

Since Jesus came into history, eyewitnesses are needed. John says 'we beheld'. Those who have claimed Christ never existed ignore the evidence. The Christians have seen a 'visible' God. This is an amazing claim.

If true, it is fantastic. Do we question it? Has the reality made its impact on us? The more profound the theology, the more far-reaching its practical effects. We can never exhaust the constant challenge of God becoming man.

JOHN 1:19–34
Profile of a man of God

*All the gospels tell us about John the Baptist.
His claim to fame is that he was a herald to
Jesus. In this passage he talks about himself
and about his relation to the coming Messiah.*

He disclaims the Messianic Office
People were expecting the Messiah. John was clearly a
striking character in his animal skins and uncompromising
preaching. They could easily have mistaken him for the
Messiah. But he dismisses the possibility.

He accepts a most lowly office
He was neither Elijah nor the prophet, both people who
were widely expected to come. Instead he was no more
than a voice. He used the language of Isaiah. He was not
even a prominent voice – he cried out in a desert rather than
in a city. This speaks highly of his humility.

He announces the presence of one much greater
He answers the Pharisees' question about his baptism by
pointing to Christ. He was unworthy to take off his sandals
– the lowliest task. Was there another of greater character
than John? The hearers were left in no doubt.

He reveals the true nature of the Messiah's mission
He makes several statements about Jesus:
>   He was the Lamb of God come to deal with sin.
>   He ranked higher that John himself.
>   He was made known to John through the Spirit.
>   He was to baptise with the Spirit.

*Jesus described John as the greatest born of
woman. Yet he was a man of remarkable
humility. We shall never have a task as
honoured as his, but we can and should covet
his gift of self-effacement.*

JOHN 1:29
The Lamb of God

*We have here the first public witness to Jesus.
It is quite unexpected. We might have thought
that the herald of Jesus would proclaim him as
Messiah or as King or even as Saviour. Why
the strange figure of a Lamb? There is clearly
more in this than meets the eye.*

The Lamb is worthy to look at

This is no ordinary statement. Neither the speaker nor the
subject was ordinary. Yet only the speaker has so far stood
out. Nobody had stopped to look at Jesus in the crowd.
John draws attention to him. This is the function that all
Christians have had ever since. When the hearers looked at
Jesus, what did they think?

The Lamb is identified with Jesus

Jewish hearers would be familiar with the religious idea of
the lamb. At Passover time all Jewish households were
acutely conscious of the lamb to be offered.

It pointed back to the deliverance from Egypt. The feast
of the Passover would remind the people of God's act on
their behalf. But where does Jesus come in? Some might
have thought of the lamb in Isa. 53. This Lamb was unique.
He was not an animal, but a person.

The Lamb was God's provision

At the Passover the householder provided the lamb. Here
God does. This idea is a mystery, but reminds us man could
never have provided as adequate a Lamb as God has done.

God's Lamb was unique in that he shared God's nature.
The gospel has already made this clear. He was not *a* Lamb
but *the* Lamb of God.

The Lamb deals with man's sin

The Old Testament sacrifices related to sin. Since similar
language is used, the statement here should be understood
in a similar sense. Jesus had come to be a sacrifice for sins.

25

John the Baptist announces only the fact. He does not describe the method.

Note the completeness of the removal. There is no suggestion of the need for repetition as with the old sacrifices. Note also the extent of the removal – the sins of the world. Jesus' mission was to be universal, effective for both Jew and Gentile alike.

The invitation still stands. To look towards the Lamb is possible for everyone. Those who look will appreciate why the Lamb is worshipped in Rev. 5.

JOHN 1:35–42
The guests of Jesus

Jesus had no settled home, but his temporary quarters were used to good effect. This passage shows the hospitality of Jesus.

The background
Two disciples of John the Baptist had been well prepared, having heard Jesus proclaimed as the Lamb of God. They were drawn to Jesus and decided to follow him.

The meeting
Jesus asks a question which draws out a response. He had taken the initiative. Their response was modest, perhaps a little self-conscious – where was he living? Jesus at once gives an invitation and provides a gracious lesson in personal relationships.

The visit
It happened at 4.00 p.m., according to the Jewish reckoning. It no doubt lasted some hours. No indication is given of what was said. In view of verse 41 some explanation of what Jesus had come to do must surely have been given.

The sequel

They were convinced that Jesus was the Messiah for whom many in Israel were looking. They were equally convinced that this news was worth spreading. Andrew brings back Peter, and Jesus at once pronounces him to be a rock. So began the band of Jesus' disciples.

The welcome of Jesus to come and see still stands. It forms a pattern for those who would spread the good news. It suggests the important place of hospitality in contacting others.

JOHN 1:40–42
Andrew: a brother who cared

Here is a man whose family relationships led to the establishing of even closer spiritual relationships.

He discovered a most important truth

(a) He powerfully summed it up in the words, 'We have found the Messiah'.

(b) He had no doubt his brother would know what he meant. Today more explanations have to be given. But this is still the most significant discovery that anyone can make. It needs to be expressed in intelligible terms.

He shared the news with his brother

He lost no time in finding Simon. The latter appears to have been the stronger personality. But it is clear that a strong bond existed between the two brothers. Andrew had no desire to keep his discovery to himself.

He brought his brother to Jesus

He took active steps to ensure a face-to-face experience. Talking is one thing. But so much more effective is action

27

which exposes others directly to the influence of Jesus. This experience led to the making of a significant disciple.

He saw the reward of his brotherly devotion

(a) He was there when Jesus told Simon, 'You are Cephas'. It would not have meant so much then as it did later. Andrew was also present at Caesarea Philippi when Jesus expanded on the same theme.

(b) Probably neither brother grasped the meaning at this point, but Andrew could not have missed the fact that Jesus highly regarded Peter on his first acquaintance with him.

The application to our present experience is not hard to see. Family associations often present particular opportunities for the sharing of the gospel.

JOHN 1:43–51
Nathanael

It is fascinating to discover how different people come to Jesus. No two are alike, yet each is instructive. We shall note the stages of Nathanael's contact with Jesus.

He had a valuable friend

We know that Philip had already found Jesus. He had decided to respond to the invitation of Jesus to follow him. He was very much a beginner but was able to share some vital information:

Jesus of Nazareth the son of Joseph was the one promised in the law and prophets.

This was an extraordinary statement, and Nathanael has some hesitations. Out of Nazareth? But his friend was a faithful witness, and his words overcame the doubts.

He was a man without guile

He made the most of his opportunities. Jesus at once noted his qualities.

(a) *His lack of guile.* This was not a common quality. It contrasts with the craftiness of Jacob. Few escape from a measure of inward scheming. How refreshing it is to meet a man without it!

(b) *His enquiring mind.* How do you know me? This is a salutary reminder that Jesus knows people before they know him.

(c) *His meditative nature.* He was under the fig tree for a purpose, perhaps to reflect on the Scriptures. He was probably a pious man, who had been noted by Jesus.

He was a man with a high view of Jesus

(a) *Rabbi.* He appreciated that Jesus bore comparison with the religious teachers. But Nathanael saw more than a good teacher.

(b) *Son of God.* It is amazing that he so quickly detected this. He saw more than an ordinary man, whatever he understood by the title he used.

(c) *King of Israel.* Nathanael was possibly thinking in nationalistic terms. The concept would move on to a more spiritual plane later. But it was certainly a recognition of sovereignty.

He was a man with a great future

Greater things are in store. Jesus promised a development in his faith. He would see what Jacob dreamed happening to the Son of Man, by which Jesus must have been referring to himself. In both cases there was direct communication between heaven and earth in the form of ascending and descending angels. Nathanael was to see this being worked out in the life of Jesus.

Follow Nathanael's example and discover what greater things Jesus will make known. 'Come and see' is a continuing invitation.

JOHN 2:1–11
Water into wine

Jesus was no mere miracle worker. He had power to perform miracles, but always used that power for a specific purpose. This incident illustrates his approach.

Jesus sanctifies a time of joy

A significant commencement to a ministry which was to end in the sorrow of the cross. This contrasts with the austerity of John the Baptist. But note that Jesus' presence was in response to an invitation. He did not gatecrash. He respected the rights of others.

Jesus faces an embarrassing situation

The no-wine situation would be an insult at an eastern festivity. Jesus appears to give a harsh response to his mother – yet not so harsh in Greek as in English. Perhaps she had been officious. She had no right to tell him what to do.

His hour was not yet. The first reminder of a climax which was to come later (cf. 12:23).

Jesus supplies a need

A miracle proceeded on the basis of obedience to Jesus' command. Mary had grasped this principle. The water jars were large and the proposal therefore suggests an ample supply.

We are not told what the servants thought as they poured in water. Note the sequence – fill, draw out, take.

Jesus astounds the steward

Jesus was not following normal practice. Some like the steward can think only in terms of the normal. Worldly wisdom acts on the principle of deterioration; Jesus on the principle of progress.

His policy is always to keep better things in store.

Jesus uses his power for God's glory

The first of the signs showed the glory of Jesus, but 1:14 has already shown that glory to belong to the Father. It led the disciples to believe. The miracles of Jesus are never an end in themselves. This gospel sees them essentially as signs.

At a simple rustic wedding Jesus transformed the scene. His presence still enhances every situation where he is invited to be present.

JOHN 2:1–11
Jesus and the natural world

The writer records a miracle without drawing attention to its supernatural character. He almost relates it as normal. But it tells something of Jesus' approach to the natural world.

Jesus demonstrates his command of nature

No explanation is given as to the processes by which the water became wine. Speculations are not profitable. The incident was intended to demonstrate an abnormal event.

Jesus used human agents in performing the miracle

The water pots had to be filled. Man was co-operating with God. Even supernatural power often moves along human channels. This is a principle with widespread applications.

Jesus used existing materials

He did not create new jars, nor fill the empty jars with wine. He used what was there. Whenever divine power operates, it works in an existing situation to change what already exists.

Jesus transforms the natural state

Water is the basis of wine, not vice versa. Jesus miraculously hastens the natural process. This miracle does not undermine nature by going against it, but shows perfect control over it.

Jesus' action suggests that nature is for man's benefit
He commanded nature to give of its best. This act should be contrasted with Jesus' refusal to turn stones into bread (a totally unnatural process) for his own benefit.

Those who deny to Jesus the power to perform miracles make him a captive of the natural order. Yet his life and death are seen as the breaking through of the divine into the human, and some supernatural events are not to be thought impossible in the light of this.

JOHN 2:1–11
Jesus and the married state

It is striking after the lofty introduction to Jesus in John 1 that the first public act is at a village wedding. The incarnate Word is seen at once in a down to earth human situation. This shows something of Jesus' view of marriage.

His presence endorsed the marriage rite
His presence at the wedding shows that he gave it his blessing. He would later teach the sanctity of marriage, but here he illustrates his support for the institution.

His presence added to the human happiness
He did not despise the festivities. He was no kill-joy. He recognised that marriage is the occasion of great happiness as two people publicly join their lives together.

The interest of Jesus in a wedding should assure us that he is deeply concerned about human relationships. He is seen as the upholder of the family unit.

JOHN 2:4
My hour is not yet

*Jesus knows that his life is planned. His hour
is his destiny. That destiny pointed to his
death. His approach to his life's work is a
pattern for us.*

No event happens by accident
The New Testament clearly teaches that Jesus was sent by
God. His mission was not his own. Everything he did he did
in conscious obedience to the Father's will. The 'hour' was
the climax to his act of obedience.

What was true of Jesus is equally true for his followers.
Our task is to follow out the divine pattern.

Each event brought the hour nearer
John reiterates the 'not yet' theme throughout the gospel.
It adds a sense of dignified progress to the record. Jesus was
acutely aware that his times were in the hands of God, even
at a wedding feast. This shows the serenity which should
mark the Christian's approach to the march of time.

Each event must be seen in the light of the climax
The hour did not take long to come for Jesus, but his mind
was geared to it right from the start. For all men life is
relatively short. It is incumbent on us to use what time we
have in the light of the final reckoning.

Each event should be used for God's glory
Although the significant hour was not yet, the present hour
was used to good account. The disciples saw glory and
discovered faith. This is a reminder that God's glory is the
yardstick by which to measure the success or failure of the
present.

*Those whose lives are totally committed to
God can learn to adopt the same dedication as
Jesus in detecting the purpose of God in each
succeeding event.*

JOHN 2:5
Do whatever He tells you

*Not much of what Mary said has been
recorded. Here is a piece of amazingly sound
advice. Although given for a specific occasion
its relevance is continual.*

Advice based on knowledge of Jesus
Such complete commitment to anyone must have a solid
basis. Mary knew something about Jesus' power and in-
tegrity. We are privileged to know more. In view of the
revelation of his status as God's son, the advice is all the
more necessary.

Advice which needed to be followed meticulously
His methods were unorthodox. The servants might have
been excused for questioning them. But they did not. They
became as a result a pattern of obedience for us. The New
Testament nowhere weakens this demand for implicit
obedience.

*One of the most difficult lessons to learn is to
obey. We tend to think we know better. But
Mary's advice makes no allowance for our
opinions.*

JOHN 2:12
A few days in Capernaum

*These few days were transitional. The public
ministry is about to begin. We may wonder
why John includes this brief note.*

The location
Capernaum was to become an important place in the

ministry of Jesus. Yet it was a hard place against which he was later to utter a warning (Matt. 11:23, 24). Did he realise this during those few days? He deliberately made his home there after leaving Nazareth (Matt. 4:13).

The occasion

It followed the wedding at Cana. The first disciples and the family of Jesus were together. His brothers and sisters did not believe, but Jesus did not turn his back on them. He recognised the force of family ties. Later he rejected advice that his brothers tried to give him (Jn. 7:3ff). Yet they too came to believe (Acts 1:14). The seeds were being sown in this quiet few days at Capernaum.

> *Relatives may be hard to influence for Christ, but the positive approach which Jesus took towards his own family provides an example and encouragement.*

JOHN 2:13–22
The Father's honour

The temple stands for the worship of God. It represents the religious practices of the time. The cleansing of the temple is therefore symbolic as well as actual. It is significantly placed at the beginning of the ministry. It shows Jesus' concern for his Father's honour.

Wrath against dishonour

The temple was claimed to be the house of God. But Jesus sees it as a place of dubious business. The money changers were extortioners. Immoral trading was going on in God's house and this was against the honour of God.

The action Jesus took was drastic. To drive out the offenders with a home-made whip was a tour de force which shows the dominating power of righteous indignation. This was an unusual role for Jesus.

Dishonour's futile defence

The authorities show no awareness of the justice of Jesus' action. They ask for a sign. The request appears absurd in face of the demonstration of Jesus' authority. Men are always wanting to challenge God and they did so throughout the ministry of Jesus.

The answer presented an enigma. Jesus' promise to rebuild the Temple in three days was unintelligible to them.

  (a) They would never destroy their own temple;
  (b) It had already taken forty-six years in building, and a three days re-erection was manifestly absurd;
  (c) They were in no state to detect any deeper significance. Even the disciples failed to do this.

The true sign vindicated the Father's honour

The disciples later recognised a clear allusion to the resurrection. This was God's own answer to the needs of his people, so poignantly illustrated in the deficiencies in the temple worship. It took the resurrection to convince the disciples. Most of the religious leaders even then failed to understand.

We would expect to find the highest expression of religious faith in the temple. But this incident shows its discovery elsewhere by simple people as a result of a stupendous event.

JOHN 2:17
Consuming zeal

An Old Testament statement is here illustrated by an event in the life of Jesus. It came to mind as the disciples reflected on the cleansing of the Temple. It focuses on a passion for God.

Spiritual zeal has a special intensity

The highest kind of zeal has as its object concern for the

purity of the house of God and all it stands for. Such zeal springs from the depths of man's spiritual life. It springs from his relationship with God.

Wherever God is worshipped is his 'house' and that is a hallowed place. Jesus was not here concerned merely for a building, but for the whole manner of worship. He saw the temple as representing his Father's house and this conviction was the source of his zeal.

Spiritual zeal reacts strongly to spiritual abuses

Jesus saw the place of worship reduced to a place of merchandise. The spiritual and the material had become indistinguishable. Such confusion is an ever present reality. It demands strong action if the spiritual is to overcome the inroads of the secular.

The zeal of Jesus is a prototype. It does not tolerate compromise. No negotiations were permissible with the abusers of God's house.

Spiritual zeal needs sometimes to take strong action

Jesus expressed his zeal in a dramatically forceful way. His was no weak approach, but action backed by moral indignation. His disciples must not shirk the call to strong action where this is demanded by the circumstances.

The zeal was also uncompromising. Everyone and everything was implicated. Was this too drastic? The disciples did not think so when they remembered the consuming passion of the Psalmist.

The consequences of the zeal were undoubtedly heroic. It was a demonstration of high courage to challenge the *status quo*. It always is.

History is full of heroic acts of zeal in the service of God in face of strong resistance. The cause of God continually needs these demonstrations of righteous indignation. Are we holding back where more zealous action is demanded?

JOHN 2:19
Jesus and his own death

*Throughout his ministry Jesus gives hints of
his awareness of his own approaching death.
The almost incidental statement here is
significant in throwing light on what he
thought about his destiny.*

He saw his body as a temple
It is not surprising that his hearers did not understand. But
what did he mean?

A temple is a dwelling place of God. At least that is its
aim. John says in 1:14 that the Word, that is God, dwelt
among us. There is a mystery here. God was dwelling in
Jesus as in a temple. His body was the human habitation of
God. This is worth pondering even if we cannot fathom it.

He realised men would destroy his body
In the Synoptic gospels Jesus several times predicted the
fact that he would die. It did not take him by surprise.
Although his hearers did not understand his invitation, the
religious representatives were later to initiate the destruction. It happened at Calvary in the cruellest manner that
man could devise.

He predicted the resurrection of the body
Even if his hearers had penetrated the meaning, they would
not have grasped the possibility of the resurrection. It took
the event itself to convince the disciples. Jesus never regarded his death as the end. In him death was to receive a
fatal blow.

*Centuries later people still dispute the
resurrection. But it still forms a central part of
the Christian message.*

JOHN 2:23–25
The first Passover Feast

The Jewish feasts are important in this gospel.
They show Jesus in relation to the religious life
of his people. The Passover is especially
significant because it was at such a feast that
Jesus died.

A time of great opportunity
Jerusalem was thronged and Jesus chose this occasion to
perform many signs. Only John records a visit to the capital
as early as this. But he sees the witness of Jesus in Jerusalem
to be of great importance.

A time of apparent response
A miracle worker always causes a stir. Many were convinced by the miracles. They believed in his name, which
seems to mean that they saw the signs as evidences of the
Messiah. But Jesus had come to do more than perform
miracles. John notes the character of the response to
remind his readers of this.

A time for caution
Jesus distrusted the reaction. He was not canvassing for
admirers of his miraculous powers, but for those who would
understand his mission.

A time for understanding
It dawned on John, no doubt later, that Jesus had an
uncanny understanding of other people. He tells us that
Jesus' insight was independent of the advice of others. His
understanding penetrates to the depths of the mind.

The insight of Jesus is amply illustrated in
many of the incidents recorded in the gospel,
not least in the meeting with Nicodemus which
comes next.

JOHN 3:1-15
Jesus talks to Nicodemus

We know little of Nicodemus. But what we do know is instructive. He was in some ways a special case. He was one of the few Jewish leaders desirous of knowing about Jesus.

His religious background

(a) Nicodemus was a Pharisee, a member of the most pious of the religious parties. He was evidently a deeply religious man.

(b) He was one of the leaders. This is probably why he came by night. It needed much moral courage to seek out the wisdom of a teacher not recognised by the schools. The fact that he came is more important than the way that he came.

His estimate of Jesus

(a) He recognised him as a teacher. The title Rabbi was an honoured title. Most of his contemporaries regarded Jesus as untaught, but in some way Nicodemus had more wisdom. He believed that Jesus was sent from God.

(b) He was impressed by his signs. Many others were also impressed, as 2:23 shows. But he went beyond them in his quest for more knowledge.

His confrontation with Jesus

His carefully prepared opening speech is cut short. Jesus takes the initiative, and gives Nicodemus a direct challenge. Rebirth is needed – otherwise there is no hope of seeing the kingdom of God.

(a) He misunderstands the nature of rebirth. He can think only in terms of natural birth, which makes nonsense of the idea of rebirth. It is not clear whether Nicodemus has a serious problem, or whether he is taking evasive action.

(b) He needs the same advice repeated. But note the differences. Here the agency of the Spirit, and entry into (rather than just seeing) the kingdom of God are mentioned. Jesus adds a further explanation of the difference between flesh and Spirit. The illustration from the wind highlights the difficulty of understanding.

(c) He puts a further question and receives a mild rebuke for it. A teacher in Israel should not be as clueless as this man turns out to be. Reading between the lines, we can detect Nicodemus' embarrassment. He had met his match and was baffled.

He was given an exposition of heavenly truth

It is not clear where the interview ended. But it may well have extended to verse 15.

Jesus claims authority to teach. Note the 'truly, truly', and the claim to know. In spite of his opening remarks, Nicodemus was not ready to receive the testimony of Jesus. Nevertheless he must have done so at a later stage (cf. 7:50; 19:39).

The heavenly things of which Jesus speaks involved teaching about the son of Man and his ascension; Moses and the serpent seen as a type of uplifting; and the connection between faith and eternal life. These words have been pondered for centuries – it is small wonder that Nicodemus found them difficult.

Nicodemus must have treasured his nocturnal interview with Jesus. He probably retold the details to the writer of the gospel. We may be grateful for the inclusion of the report here, for it is still pregnant with meaning and challenge.

JOHN 3:7, 8
New birth

*There is an air of mystery about any birth.
The idea of spiritual birth is no different. It
draws attention to the wonder of new life.
Jesus' statement still causes the same
bewilderment as it originally did.*

An amazing declaration
Jesus confronts a Jewish religious leader. He wanted to
know, but his mind found it difficult to grasp. To be born
again was not everyday language. If a man like Nicodemus
was perplexed, who can be expected to understand?

A Jewish leader would no doubt have connected it with
renewal. But the problem was to grasp that he himself
needed it.

A divine imperative
'You must' leave no room for compromise. Choice is out of
the question. Two things are clear:
 (a) The natural man cannot dispense with it.
 (b) It cannot be achieved by an external rite. Spiritual
     regeneration is indispensable.

A mysterious operation
Jesus illustrates this point from the wind. Wind and spirit
are closely connected.

Man can control neither. He can see neither. Both are
unpredictable. Even with modern technology to plot the
winds, unexpected changes not infrequently occur.

Spirit, like wind, can be powerful in its action. The
parallel impresses us with the mystery of rebirth.

An unmistakable evidence
Wind is most widely known by its effects. We do not need to
prove its presence. Similarly conversion shows itself in
changed lives. God is not stereotyped in his actions. His
dealing with people is as varied as the varieties of the
wind.

A personal directive

The words are not simply addressed to Nicodemus. The plural is used. This kind of rebirth is a necessity for everyone. No one can escape the need to apply the words to himself.

The demand of Jesus is not outdated. Human need remains unchanged. New birth is not an optional extra, but is essential for all who would find God.

JOHN 3:8
Wind and Spirit

The natural elements are often used in Scripture to illustrate spiritual truths. God is described as the Sun; the righteous are described as flourishing trees. One of the more vivid is the wind to express the work of the Spirit.

The mystery of its origin

It is sovereign in its operation. Man cannot control the approaching hurricane. He takes shelter and waits.

The sovereignty of the Spirit is more remarkable than the wind. He was present at the first creation as he is at all subsequent creative acts. He acts in individual conversions and in mass revivals.

The mystery of its characteristics

(a) *Its invisibility*. We cannot see the wind, only its effects. Sometimes the Spirit works quietly, sometimes strongly. The Spirit, like God the Father, is invisible. Beware of dispensing with what cannot be seen. It would be as foolish as refusing to use electricity.

(b) *Its incomprehensibility*. Much is now known about the wind through modern technology. But advances in science have not illuminated the Spirit's working. We cannot analyse his mind. The book of Acts tells us what he did, not how or even why.

The mystery of his power
Wind can be gentle, but can also be wild. It can be soothing or destructive. It illustrates the variety of the Spirit's operations. But God's Spirit is never arbitrary or capricious. He does not harm. He brings blessing and renewal.

We live in an era of the Spirit. We should allow the Spirit to move as he chooses in our lives.

JOHN 3:14, 15
Symbol and salvation

Symbols are valuable for conveying spiritual truths. Here an Old Testament symbol is applied in a new way.

The nature of the symbol
It is based on a historic event. Moses' action is referred to in Numb. 21:7–9. The Brass Snake was not responsible for the miracle. God's power was behind the healing properties of a sight of it.

The event pointed to a future fulfilment. Jesus recognised in it a symbol of himself.

The interpretation of the symbol
Jesus identifies the serpent with the Son of Man, his favourite name for himself. He had come from heaven (verse 13). But the title points to his humanity.

The lifting up is fulfilled in the cross. Here Jesus gives some clue to explain his death.

The application of the symbol

As the Israelites looked and lived, so men must now believe to receive a superior form of life – eternal life.

As everyone who looked lived, so everyone who believes receives eternal life. This is the only condition Jesus demands. Cf. Isa. 45:22 here.

Symbols always point to a greater reality beyond them. The reality in this case is at the heart of the gospel.

JOHN 3:16–30
The intention of God's love

It is not clear whether these verses continue Jesus' teaching to Nicodemus, or whether they are John's own comments. Either way they sum up the gospel.

The design of the Incarnation

The positive side – eternal life rather than destruction. The negative side – condemnation for the unbelieving.

The motive for the Incarnation

It springs from God's love. Love gave its best – the beloved Son. The description is repeated for emphasis. Such love is indescribable.

The scope of the Incarnation

The object of God's love was the world. Yet eternal life is narrowed to those who believe. God's salvation is both comprehensive and conditional.

The result of the Incarnation

Because the Light has shone and men loved darkness, condemnation is unavoidable. Men's evil deeds were already present, but the Incarnation leaves those who do them without excuse.

45

Here Light and Love are linked. The doings
of Love have nothing to hide. The Incarnation
has brought a new dimension into the world –
living by the truth.

JOHN 3:16
The greatness of God's love

This is a favourite verse because of what it tells
us about God. It is impossible to describe
God's love except in terms of what he has
done.

Its object
The 'world' may seem very general, but it expresses the
wide scope of God's love. In John it describes fallen
mankind – man in revolt against God – man deserving
punishment. It was a most unattractive object.

Its gift
Love always delights to give. The intensest love wants to
give its best. God's one and only Son was that best gift.
God's love was sacrificial in the extreme.

Its achievement
It prevents destruction. A fallen world deserved this fate.
It secures eternal life. Love wants the objects of its love
to be ever present.

Its vehicle
It is appropriated through faith. It makes sense only to the
believer. We cannot command God's love, but we can
accept it.

This verse has been called the gospel in a
nutshell. Its relevance is only plain for those
who exist in a fallen world. God could justly
have destroyed, but instead he saves.

JOHN 3:17
God's mission to save

Our view of God is of utmost importance. Do we think of him as judgmental? Have we grasped his true design for mankind? This verse sets it out clearly.

What it is not
It is not for condemnation. Man could not have complained if it had been. It would only have been what he deserved. But God is no tyrant. His purpose was quite different.

What it is
It is to save. Salvation is the content of the gospel. God was doing something in Christ which man could not do. It was centred in history – in the incarnation.

We often need the negative to appreciate the positive. It shows us what God is like. His desires are for man's good. Any lesser view of him is untrue to the Gospel message.

JOHN 3:18, 19
The Christian alternative

We are constantly faced with choices. Our decisions often have far reaching consequences. But none is more crucial than our attitude to God's gift of Christ.

Faith versus unbelief
The matter is black and white. The believer is not condemned; the unbeliever is. Christ himself is the touchstone. There can be no middle way.

Unbelief is linked with darkness

Men loved darkness rather than light. This is incredible to those who have experienced the light. To choose to grope around in the dark is surely a foolish choice. Yet the unbelieving world does this and often thinks the believer to be foolish.

Faith is linked with light

It requires humility to allow light to expose one's deeds. But the alternative is even more humiliating. To admit the darkness is the cost of appreciating the light.

The choice before us allows no compromise.
Either we believe and live, or we refuse to
believe and stand condemned before God.

JOHN 3:22–30
John and Jesus

John the Baptist has already testified to Jesus
in this gospel. Here he throws more light on
the one whose herald he was.

Controversy led to clarification

Arguments often drive people apart. But here a more positive result followed. The cause was a dispute over ceremonial washing. John's disciples were involved. But the real issue was John's relation to Jesus.

John refutes any suggestion of competition

He had made quite clear that he was not the Messiah. He understood both his own role and that of Jesus. He takes the trouble to resolve his disciples' perplexity.

John sees himself as the friend of the bridegroom

The wedding imagery is suggestive. The bride is undefined, but links up with the bride as the church (Eph. 5:25ff; Rev.

19:6ff). Christ is the Bridegroom and John takes the lowlier place as his friend. He delights to hear the Bridegroom's voice.

John recognises his own decreasing role

His statement is relevant to all God's servants. The increase of Christ and decrease of self is a perpetual Christian principle.

> *John the Baptist provides a timeless example of true selflessness. He is not bugged by self-importance. Here is a profitable lesson for all Christian workers.*

JOHN 4:1–6
Jesus changes direction

> *This section involves a change of plans. It is instructive to note the reasons given. They may suggest some useful principles for guidance.*

He knew what was in the minds of the Pharisees

The text simply says he knew that the Pharisees had heard. But he also knew the implications of this. It would arouse jealousy.

He left Judea to avoid an unnecessary clash

It was not fear of the Pharisees, but wisdom in deciding the most appropriate action. Cf. Jesus' advice to his disciples (Mt. 10:23).

He decided to go through Samaria

The text implies some form of compulsion. Jesus always saw God's plan in what he did. It would have been easier for him as a Jew to avoid Samaria.

He came to a historic place
It was not so much Sychar as Jacob's well that was renowned. But the well was to become even more renowned
after the visit of Jesus.

He arrived at the heat of the day
The sixth hour was midday. The time of greatest heat and
greatest weariness. This circumstance prepared the way for
a historic event.

*Sometimes God's plans seem more than
surprising. But Jesus was fully prepared for
what was to follow.*

JOHN 4:7–14
Jesus and the Samaritan woman

*Jesus shows the way to lead another to the
truth. Here is a perfect example of personal
communication. It also raises the issues of
thirst and of racism, so relevant in today's
world.*

Jesus meets a needy person
  (a) The person was a *woman*. Consider this against the
      background of the poor view of women in the
      ancient world. Jews segregated women from men.
      The emancipation of women is part of the triumph of
      Christianity.
  (b) The woman was a *Samaritan*. Most Jews would have
      spurned her. She was in their eyes inferior.
  (c) The woman was evidently *socially ostracised*. She
      drew water at noon which others would avoid. She
      was an adulteress.

Jesus takes the initiative
Jesus asks for a drink. He puts the ball in her court. His
request shows he himself has a need. But she would never

have offered a drink to a Jew. Jesus overrode current conventions in order to communicate.

Jesus faces a racial problem
His action immediately raises an issue of race. She recognised his Jewishness. Her prejudices were awakened. It created genuine perplexity. Was there really a way to overcome the racial and religious barrier?

Jesus makes an offer
Having asked for a drink, Jesus now offers one. But the switch was difficult for the woman. There was the deepness of the well; the absence of a bucket; the problem of Jacob's greatness; the ignorance of the true nature of Jesus; the misunderstanding over 'living' water.

The woman represents that class of materially minded people who have unrecognised spiritual needs.

Jesus gives an explanation
He explains the superiority of what he offers.
   (a) It satisfies more than immediate needs. The physical water could only temporarily quench thirst. Living water permanently meets the longing of the soul.
   (b) It comes from an inexhaustible supply. Drought can never affect it – it comes from God's resources.
   (c) It has an abundant effect. It wells up to eternal life. It is like a tumbling stream which cannot be contained.

The woman asks for water – but has still not grasped the difference. But the desire had been awakened in another for something which really satisfies. It requires personal skill to help others to transfer from material to spiritual ideas.

JOHN 4:10
If you knew

*The words imply a lack of knowledge.
Curiosity is the means that Jesus uses to turn
the conversation.*

What she failed to understand

(a) The gift of God. He is constantly giving, but this is a special gift – spiritual satisfaction.

(b) The identity of Jesus. Ignorance of who he is can have disastrous consequences.

What she consequently failed to ask

(a) The living water was available for the asking. In this case she gained it through the prompting of Jesus.

(b) How often ignorance prevents people enjoying the benefits of the gospel!

*Think how much we miss because we have not
bothered to find out. How sad that
opportunities for spiritual blessing slip past. If
only we had known!*

JOHN 4:15–20
Jesus turns the conversation

*It is often difficult to steer a conversation in a
spiritual direction. Here the master
communicator shows us how to do it.*

The woman presents an opportunity

She was asking for water to avoid the daily trek to the well. But Jesus introduces a counter-question which answers only indirectly.

Jesus shows knowledge of her past

The 'husband' question was to draw attention to her spiritual condition. She had a moral problem and is surprised at Jesus' knowledge of it. But she did at least admit it.

Jesus draws out an acknowledgment about himself

The prophet status was not particularly advanced, but it was a start. She realised Jesus was different. He had amazing perception.

Jesus confronts a religious problem

The clash between Jews and Samaritans was historic. The woman may have been trying to deflect the conversation, or expressing a genuine problem. But it raised the importance of worshipping God.

At the end of this part of the dialogue the talk had reached serious issues. We note the skill with which Jesus had achieved this.

JOHN 4:21–24
Acceptable worship

Worship and its modes are a universal subject of interest. Here Jesus throws considerable light on what God finds acceptable.

Worship must be universal

Jesus rejects merely localised worship. Whether at Gerizim, the Samaritan's sacred mount, or Jerusalem, the Jewish centre, makes no difference.

People find it easier to rely on sacred places. But this misses the true spirit of worship. It must be independent of locality.

Worship must be to God as Father

It was the aim of Jesus to throw light on the Fatherhood of God. The Jews had more light on this than the Samaritans, for salvation was of the Jews – the Messiah was to come from such a source. But both had more to learn.

Worship must take a spiritual form

Since God is Spirit, nothing other than spiritual worship is acceptable. This involves the help of the Holy Spirit. This is not a future dream, but was happening in the ministry of Jesus. Indeed Jesus himself provides the pattern for the church.

Here is deep truth revealed to an insignificant woman. It is a lesson as relevant to modern civilisation. The spiritual dimension is all too often ousted out.

JOHN 4:23, 24
True worshippers

Some form of worship is a universal quest. But much of it does not satisfy or achieve its end. Here Jesus makes clear what true worship is.

Whom we should worship

Clearly this is the most important question. Jesus gives two indications.
(a) *God as Spirit.* This would run counter to all kinds of material gods.
(b) *God as Father.* No one has revealed this as vividly as Jesus. A right understanding of the Fatherhood of God transforms worship. Cf. the Lord's Prayer.

How we should worship

Methods of worship vary considerably, but two conditions must be fulfilled.
(a) *It must be in spirit.* This would contrast with mere outward ritual. It stresses the state of the heart and mind.

(b) *It must be in truth.* Here the genuineness of the action is in mind. Worshipping should find no place for pretence.

When we should worship
'The hour is coming and now is' means now and at any time. True worship is not for special occasions.

Where we should worship
Jews favoured Jerusalem, Samaritans Mount Gerizim. But neither is necessary. Worship is independent of special localities.

Why we should worship
It is not a case of our own inclination. It is because of the nature of God Himself. He seeks for worshippers.

Here is a yardstick for our worship. How do we measure up to it?

JOHN 4:25–30
Jesus makes himself known

It is rare for Jesus to identify himself openly, but he does here. We note the stages and their results.

The woman affirms her present knowledge
She recognised the importance of the Messiah, whatever she understood by that. She thought in terms of a prophet (probably from Deut. 18:18). He was to be the great revealer. This differed from the Jewish hopes of a conquering Messiah.

Jesus takes up the point to reveal himself
She had already recognised his prophetic ability. Now he claims more. Her openness of mind prepared the way. He reveals more to those who really want to know.

The woman responds by action

There is a remarkable contrast between the silence of the disciples and that of the woman. They had questions which they did not ask. She left her waterpots with a deep conviction that she had met the Messiah. She wanted others to know.

When a person has a true introduction to Jesus the first impulse is to let others know about it.

JOHN 4:27
Why a woman?

In Jesus' day women were underprivileged. Since then the gospel has done much for their emancipation. Jesus' conversation with this Samaritan woman is illuminating.

The disciples were astonished

It was against social convention for Jesus to talk with a strange woman. The disciples reflect current opinions.

Jesus was unconventional

He was concerned more for her need than for conformity to social practice. To him a woman's needs were as great as a man's. He ignored the current male-female dichotomy in religious and social life.

Jesus was undiscriminating

The woman was apparently an adulteress, for she lived with a man who was not her husband. But Jesus treats her as an individual with a spiritual need. Jewish opinion was against the spiritual equality of women with men.

The Samaritan woman represents the needs of women. The approach of Jesus has lifted the oppression against women characteristic of most religions and civilisations.

JOHN 4:31–34
Spiritual food

The disciples had gone for natural food. They found the concern of Jesus for spiritual food perplexing. Their reactions are common to most.

The superiority of spiritual over physical needs

The disciples' concern for Jesus' physical needs was good and natural. He was a true man and needed food. This passage is no passport for Christian neglect of the body.

Yet there are other claims which take precedence. It is a question of priorities. Consider when physical needs can be temporarily set aside.

The difficulty of appreciating the spiritual food of Jesus

It was mysterious. The disciples were ignorant of it. They were thinking only of physical food. How easy it is to make the same mistake. Nicodemus confused the spiritual with the physical and most people do the same.

Spiritual food defined as doing the will of God

Jesus appeals to his mission. He was sent from God. His plan was to do God's will. He aimed to bring it to completion. In this Jesus furnishes a pattern for all believers. Nothing short of God's will satisfies.

A right understanding of spiritual food involves some shocks. Racial and religious prejudices may need overturning. An inward revolution may well be involved.

JOHN 4:34–38
The Christian harvest

Jesus often uses natural phenomena to illustrate spiritual truths. Here he penetrates the truths of spiritual productiveness through the natural harvest.

The principles of the natural harvest
Jesus refers to the crops before his eyes. He knows much has been done – the ploughing and sowing. But the harvest would not be for four months. This was common knowledge. Nothing can be done to cut down the waiting time. It was in God's hands.

The principles of the spiritual harvest
Jesus saw a different kind of reaping already to hand. He noted the Samaritans about to respond. The preparation had already been done. But the disciples' eyes did not see. It requires deep sensitivity to recognise the spiritual harvest. Was Jesus thinking here of the spread of the gospel through the whole world?

The importance of the workers
All the time God is using different agencies. Some sow and others reap. But the harvest needs to be gathered. Then all who have laboured can rejoice. In this sphere there is no competition for the reward. The spiritual harvest is the result of a concerted effort. Reaping for God is corporate not individual.

In harvesting people for God, discernment is needed to recognise ripeness. This requires an understanding of God's will. Jesus himself is the supreme example.

JOHN 4:39–42
A mass response

*An individual encounter with Jesus results in
many more coming to faith. This has
frequently been the experience of the Christian
church. It is always an encouragement when
many respond.*

Many believed because of the testimony of the woman
They did not reject her testimony because she was an
adulteress. They accepted the report of Jesus' superior
powers of understanding. Her words must have had a ring
of truth.

Many more believed the direct testimony of Jesus
The Samaritans did something about it. They came to
Jesus. They persuaded him to stay with them. Their faith
had overcome their racial prejudices. To hear his own
words was even better than the woman's testimony.

**Their belief blossomed into an acceptance
of the Saviour**
The woman had got as far as Jesus the Prophet. But the
townspeople had recognised the Saviour. Whatever their
understanding, it was penetrating enough to see the work
of Jesus in universal terms.

*The conviction of the Samaritans has been
amply confirmed. The spread of the gospel
has demonstrated that all, irrespective of race
or creed, can experience salvation.*

JOHN 4:42
The Saviour of the world

*Recognition of Jesus as Saviour is the most
far-reaching discovery anyone can make. It
does not depend on privilege or education or
race.*

It was made by the despised Samaritans
It is remarkable that they had such grasp in view of the
obstinacy of the Jews and even the dullness of the disciples,
neither of which groups arrived at the truth as early as this.

It was the result of a woman's testimony
Although she was in all probability a social outcast, they
listened to her remarkable story. Personal testimony leads
more people to the Saviour than any other means.

It constituted an adequate understanding
In spite of their lack of background in the Scriptures, these
Samaritans arrived at an essential understanding of Jesus.
They saw him not only as their Saviour, but also the
universal Saviour. It took the Christian church some years
to reach such a universal idea of salvation.

*When men are open to the truth, it need take
little time to reach a comprehensive
understanding of Christian salvation.*

JOHN 4:43–54
The growth of a man's faith in Galilee

This is more than a notable miracle. It is an account of the flowering of a man's faith in Jesus. It contains many practical lessons.

The beginnings of faith
It was occasioned by a desperate family need. Such needs are irrespective of status. The man's royal position did not safeguard him. It was hearing about Jesus that roused the first spark of faith. Jesus' arrival in Galilee was a godsend.

The approach of faith
It involved action. He went himself to Jesus. And he begged him to come to his son. He clearly thought his status would have some influence with Jesus.

The rebuke of faith
Why was Jesus so discouraging? He perceived an inadequate approach to miracles. He implied that the man's faith would not blossom until he had seen the healing. How many are guilty of the same immaturity?

The reward of faith
The nobleman was not put off. He repeated the request for Jesus to come. Faith was becoming more urgent. To this Jesus makes a positive suggestion – 'go on your own for the healing has taken place'.

The development of faith
He might have been disappointed that Jesus declined to go. But he believed that healing had happened. This was clearly the result of his encounter with Jesus.

The confirmation of faith
The nobleman meets his servants on the way and learns that his son is healed. All the details, even the time, confirms his

faith. As a consequence he commits himself to believe in Jesus.

The spread of faith
The whole household believes. Faith is infectious. Where whole households believe the witness is doubly powerful.

In face of this spectacular growth of faith, how far has the development of our faith reached? Has it stopped at the miraculous? Or has it become personal?

JOHN 5:1–9
The healing of an impotent man

Here is another sign which speaks volumes about Jesus Christ. He seeks out a distressing case, and shows the breadth of his sympathies.

Human misery as a magnet
Many turn away because it is too demanding. Misery attracts some human compassion, but Jesus demonstrates God's compassionate response.

(a) Its concentration. Here was a multitude of misery. But each person was an individual. We can visualise the sad cavalcade approaching the Bethesda pool.

(b) Its variety. The sick, blind, lame and withered. The common denominator was human weakness.

(c) Its problems. The endless superstitious waiting only intensified the pathos of the misery. Here is a picture of frustrated human need. Yet Jesus singled out one man from the crowd.

Divine mercy confronted with particular weakness
The magnitude of mercy is gauged by its object. Perhaps Jesus chose the worst example of helplessness.

(a) He was paralysed and totally dependent on others. He is a picture of man's spiritual condition.

(b) He had probably been there longest. Thirty-eight years of frustration. His best years were now gone.
(c) He had lost hope. He seems apathetic. Unlike some he did not ask for help.

Transformation through Jesus' presence
When Jesus faces the misery, dramatic changes occur.
(a) The co-operation of the will. Jesus seeks to find out whether he wanted to be healed. This was clearly not obvious. Jesus does not force his help on the unwilling.
(b) The irrelevance of past failures. The response was negative because of the man's experience of the survival of the fittest.
(c) The inspiration of a command. To rise seemed impossible, but he did it. Mercy gave the ability to respond.
(d) The immediate effect. There was no delay. A complete miracle had been performed.

A whole new life began because one man met with Jesus. And what better day than on the Sabbath!

JOHN 5:6
The importance of the will

This man's physical healing is a parable. It illustrates the processes for spiritual healing. The question is, 'Do you want to be healed?'

God seeks man's co-operation
His healing processes are never forced on unwilling subjects. God respects our desires. But apathy can rob us of the blessings of spiritual wholeness. The sick man's response was astonishingly half-hearted.

God always responds to man's co-operation

The will in this case was weak, but was nevertheless strong enough to act. The will eventually overcame the objections.

The barrier to spiritual health is never the will of God, but the will of man. No one ever came desiring spiritual healing and was turned away.

JOHN 5:10–17
The sabbath question

The sabbath question was acute in Jesus' day. It focused on the keeping of the law. Here Jesus falls foul of the authorities because of his approach to the sabbath.

The healed man causes controversy

The carrying of the bed was the offence which outweighed the remarkable act of compassion. Legalism is incapable of flexibility.

The healed man appeals to the authority of Jesus

He was ignorant of the identity of his benefactor, but he recognised his undoubted authority.

The healed man discovers his healer

No explanation is given why Jesus slipped away. Possibly he wanted to talk with the man more privately. The message is direct. 'Do not sin any more.' A spiritual challenge immediately followed the physical healing.

The healed man tells the Jews about Jesus

No reason is given. But the result was opposition to Jesus, who at once defends his action – both he and his Father were at work. The implication is that such dynamic action overrides a narrow interpretation of the Law.

When religious practice takes precedence over human needs there is something wrong. Yet this has proved in the past and present alike a difficult position to accept. Is it a challenge to us?

JOHN 5:14
Sin and suffering

The Jews debated whether suffering was due to sin. Some Christians still discuss the same problem. Some even regard all illness as resulting from sin. How far do Jesus' words here support this?

Jesus performed healings to alleviate suffering

Clearly he aimed to create wholeness in people. He was often moved with compassion. The perfect human being was moved to act when confronted with imperfections. He reminded the man from the side of the pool that he was now healed – 'See you are well!'

But he also dealt with human sin

He recognised sin as at least a contributory cause. He commanded the man to sin no more less something worse happened. It is difficult to imagine what. Cf. the healing in Mk. 2:1–12, where Jesus forgave sins before healing.

Ceasing from sin requires human determination

Forgiveness is not enough. In this case the great danger was a continuation of the same attitude of mind. Healing involves spiritual as well as physical wholeness.

There may be no connection between some forms of suffering and sin. But in some cases there is. Then the spiritual is of paramount importance.

JOHN 5:18–23
Jesus answers the charges against him

'My Father works and I work' sums up the answer. Jesus claims equality of operation. But his opponents regarded his claims as blasphemous, and plotted to kill him. Here is Jesus' self-defence.

The Father and the Son do the same things
The Son cannot do anything apart from the Father, not because he is inferior but because both share the same intention.

The Father loves to show the Son what he is doing
Love of this intensity wants to share. There are more exciting revelations to follow. This must refer to what God would do through his Son in saving the world.

The Father and the Son both give life to the dead
The fact that the Son could raise the dead demonstrates his ability to do what God can do. This is particularly powerful in the light of the resurrection of Christ.

The Father and the Son both execute judgment
The office of judge is one of highest honour. Since the Father has given authority to the Son to judge, nothing distinguishes between them.

Jesus is claiming equality with God. The Jews object. But Jesus shows how valid it is. Do we accord to Jesus the honour due to him?

JOHN 5:22, 23
The Son becomes the judge

*This is a side of the work of Christ we tend to
forget. He did not come to judge but to save.
Yet judgment will be finally given to him.*

The qualifications of the judge

He has special authority as Son of God. He is in complete
harmony with the mind of God. He is as just as God (verse
30) and none of his judgments can be false.

But he is also Son of Man (verse 27). That means he is in
complete harmony with man and understands those he
judges.

He is appointed as judge

He is not self-appointed. He carries out the full programme
of divine judgment.

His act of judging particularly relates to the end times

Jesus speaks of the two resurrections. He will inaugurate
these resurrections. It is a comfort to the good to know that
he will judge them. But for the evil it can only spell doom.

*The thought of Jesus as judge is not daunting
for the believer, who knows he is not
condemned (cf. 3:18). But Jesus never
suggests that evil will not be judged.*

JOHN 5:24–30
The two resurrections

*The previous section saw Jesus claiming to be
judge. This develops the theme and links it
with resurrection.*

The way towards a spiritual resurrection

Believers are exempt from judgment. This kind of faith
involves recognising God as the Father of Jesus. It also
involves heeding the words of Jesus. Then eternal life takes
the place of death, as Jn.3:18 shows.

The timing of this spiritual resurrection

The hour has arrived. The event is not future. The spiritually dead are now able to hear the voice of the Son of God
and live. This happens every time anyone comes to faith in
Jesus.

The basis for this spiritual resurrection

The Father is self-sufficient. The Son is self-sufficient. The
Father has given authority to the Son. It is he who gives
eternal life. It is as certain as it can be. And our judge will
be the Son of Man, who shared our nature.

The final physical resurrection

Jesus introduces a double resurrection – to life and to
judgment. The difference will depend on deeds. But does
this mean good works? Since verse 24 already speaks of life
for believers this cannot be.

*Jesus' judgment is just, because he always
does the Father's will. It is both an
encouragement and a challenge to realise that
he will judge all men.*

JOHN 5:31–40
Witness

The Old Testament suggested that at least two witnesses were needed to support any claims. What supporting witnesses did Jesus have?

The witness of John the Baptist
While Jesus does not need man's testimony, his hearers did. John was like a lamp to point the way to another.

The witness of Jesus' own works
Jesus calls attention to his activities as witnessing to his divine mission. Those who ignored or misrepresented his works failed to detect the importance of them.

The witness of the Father
When did this take place? Certainly at his baptism. But Jesus was conscious all the time of the Father speaking through him. His opponents were deaf to this.

The witness of the Scriptures
Jesus affirms that Scripture witnesses to him. Again it was not recognised, even by those who were seeking eternal life. How easy it is to fail to get the message of God's word!

The witnesses were strong and effective. But the recipients were unwilling to accept the claims of Jesus. How ready are we to listen?

JOHN 5:39
Searching the Scriptures

Some are ignorant of the Scriptures. Some ignore them. Some superficially read them. Some search them. Some even distort them. Our attitude to them is important.

Jesus acknowledged the importance of Scripture
He frequently cited it or alluded to it. He clearly regarded it as the word of God. In this he would have agreed with his Jewish contemporaries.

He recognised the possibility of missing its message
In spite of their diligent searching, the hearers had never found the secret of eternal life. This suggests that searching is not enough. It must be done in the right way.

He affirmed the witness they bore to him
It is certainly possible to miss this. Some read the Scriptures with blinkers (cf. 2 Cor. 3:14). But the early church had no doubt that they spoke of Christ. The message of the Old Testament must be interpreted in this light. (Cf. verse 46 – 'Moses . . . wrote of me'.)

Scripture is a constant witness to Jesus Christ for those who search with the aim of finding him.

JOHN 5:41-47
The causes of unbelief

The Jews were unwilling to take Jesus at his word. Their reasons for unbelief have often been repeated.

The absence of the love of God
This was hard for religious people to accept. Yet it is often true. Jesus penetrates below the surface.

The refusal to receive the Father's testimony
Man's claims are more readily received. Many false messiahs had arisen before Jesus. But God's seal on him was unacceptable to the materially minded Jews.

The delight in self-congratulation
It is possible to be so concerned with what others think that God is left out. Yet his is the greatest glory.

The inability to listen to Moses
The accusation was in the books of the Law which the hearers claimed to uphold. But they refused to recognise that Moses wrote of Jesus. With such an attitude, unbelief is not surprising.

The most important question is still whether we believe in Jesus. We may have other reasons for unbelief. Are they any more justified?

JOHN 6:1–13
Feeding a multitude

Jesus shows compassion on a crowd. Here the miracle leads to spiritual teaching. The people are long since gone, but the truth remains.

The needs of the crowd

Not just one hungry person, but more than 5000. The mass of need accentuates the problem. This has been highlighted in the famine areas of modern times.

Jesus did not ignore physical needs, although his main concern was spiritual. Man cannot live by bread alone. In this case the people were both physically and spiritually unprepared.

The perplexity of the disciples

   (a) It arose from a challenge from Jesus.
   (b) It involved a confession of inability.
   (c) It contained one small gleam of hope.
   (d) It was accentuated by a strange command.
   (e) It shared in an exciting distribution.
   (f) It took part in a laborious collection.

The generosity of the lad

   (a) He was the only one prepared.
   (b) He alone was able to give.
   (c) He alone was willing to give.
   (d) He alone was willing to give all.
       His act enriched a multitude.

The resources of Jesus

This was the central point of the miracle.
   (a) He intended to alleviate the need.
   (b) He made use of inadequate supplies.
   (c) His resources were abundant for all.
   (d) He would not waste the surplus.

From whom do we learn most in this miracle? From the crowd, the disciples, the lad or Jesus? Our quest should lead to a higher view of Christ.

JOHN 6:12, 13
The fragments

The fragments were a testimony to the abundant supply

The miracle was an act of generosity. It is portrayed as an act of compassion for the crowds. It speaks of the abundance of God's supply. Our modern world with its acute distribution problems often forgets the generous provision. There is enough food to feed the world.

The fragments suggest an element of waste

Since the pieces had to be collected they must have been discarded by the people. What comes easily is not always fully appreciated.

The fragments collected are a testimony against waste

Jesus' concern was to teach the disciples a lesson. The miracle was adequate but not extravagant. Waste is seen as non-acceptable. Jesus would side with the adage 'Waste not, want not'.

Even fragments have value. Jesus esteems the smallest pieces as having sufficient use to be preserved.

JOHN 6:14–21
Walking on the sea

We may dismiss the incident as impossible, or as an illusion. But if so we shall miss the main purpose.

The occasion of the miracle

(a) It grew out of a misconception by the crowd. That

Jesus was a prophet was true, but they wanted to make him king.

(b) It led Jesus to withdraw to a mountain to be alone. He avoids the coercion of the crowds. His kingship was to be entirely different.

The difficulties of the disciples
(a) They were probably disappointed that Jesus declined to be king.
(b) They embarked on a boat – sent by Jesus according to Mt. 14:22. But the wind was adverse and storm conditions resulted. It is a parable of God's people.
(c) Jesus walked on water to come to their aid. But they were frightened. Why? They lacked understanding of his methods. They were unprepared for the unexpected.

The calm of Jesus
This contrasts with the storm. He was master of his environment. Order was meeting disorder. He brought words of comfort. His presence completely resolved the problem.

The miracle was physical, but the lesson is symbolic. Jesus continues to meet his people's needs in the storms of life.

JOHN 6:22–29
A multitude on the search

The spectacular always excites. A miracle promotes a thirst for other miracles. But is the quest the right quest?

The search for Jesus was outwardly energetic
The multitudes use an armada of small boats to seek for Jesus. Their resourcefulness must be commended. But curiosity was a driving force – how did you get here?

Jesus exposes their real motives

The feeding for them was not a sign but an easy meal. They had not distinguished between material and spiritual food. The Son of Man had come to do more than provide a social welfare system. God's seal was on the spiritual.

Jesus advises work for spiritual objectives

Does this mean that human effort can obtain eternal life? Jesus makes clear that eternal life is a gift, not a reward. But what does work then mean?

Jesus strangely links work with faith. God's work is to believe in Jesus. This is a total re-interpretation of work. It does not depend on effort but on commitment.

The search for Jesus is still a matter of faith.
Those without it will never find him.

JOHN 6:28, 29
The works of God

God's works are greater than man's works.
But not all set their sights on them. Self
achievement is all too satisfying. Are we
sensitive to the difference?

A commendable enquiry

What must we do to do the works of God? Assuming the question was genuine, it suggests a willingness to do something about it. The works of God are not naturally performed. We need guidance about their nature.

A challenging explanation

Jesus' answer did not suggest any action. People are always happier with something to do. But he spoke of faith – they were to believe in him. Faith instead of works has always proved difficult. It leaves us without any sense of achievement.

The greatest evidence of the works of God is in the lives of those who believe. We may say of every Christian, 'There goes a work of God'.

JOHN 6:30–40
The sign of the bread from heaven

There is a constant desire for the tangible. A sign would be something outside ourselves. We could subject it to tests to decide whether we accepted it. But it is a shock to find the signs of Jesus are not like this.

They ask for bread from heaven

They appeal to history. It had been done before, why not again? The Jews were impressed with the provision of the manna. But their request was prompted by the desire for an endless supply. Could Jesus match Moses?

Jesus explains the true bread

He switches the theme from the physical to the spiritual as he did with Nicodemus. The bread of God is different. It gives real life to the world.

They ask for this bread

But Jesus introduces another switch. He himself is the bread. They did not expect this. But Jesus says more.

    (a) He totally satisfies men's hunger.

    (b) He will receive everyone the Father gives to him.

    (c) He has come to do the Father's will.

    (d) The Father's will is to bestow eternal life.

    (e) Eternal life involves resurrection at the last day.

How essential is a right understanding of what God has provided! How many miss true satisfaction because they are seeking the wrong thing?

JOHN 6:35
I am the bread of life

*Such a claim from anyone else would be
presumptuous. But for Jesus it was not
inappropriate. Consider its significance for
mankind.*

It presumes man's need for spiritual bread
Most spend their lives in the pursuit of material food. This
is legitimate and necessary. Yet man has a spiritual hunger
and thirst to be satisfied.

It affirms that Jesus can meet that need
Natural bread satisfies only temporarily. But Jesus is a gift
from God which is eternal. He has the power to satisfy
man's deepest needs. He who comes will never hunger.

It reminds us of the Last Supper
It was bread that Jesus declared to be his broken body.
He goes on to identify the bread with his flesh. Our
participation in the Bread is mysterious but real.

*Once we partake we discover the truth of
Jesus' words. No other can compare with this
Bread.*

JOHN 6:41–59
Jewish unbelief

*This passage focuses on Jewish unbelief.
Unbelief is a universal phenomena, but that of
Jesus' contemporaries was particularly acute.
It all happened in a synagogue at Capernaum.*

Bothered by incongruity
The son of Joseph and bread from heaven did not seem to

match. The problem arose from a low view of Jesus. They knew his parents – how could he come from heaven? Unbelief often begins with wrong premises.

Ignorant of the true way to God
The Father must draw. This removes their initiative. They are not taught by men, but by God. Everything now depends on their attitude to Jesus.

Oblivious of the inadequacy of the manna
The fathers had died in the wilderness. But here is food which satisfies for ever. By comparison, the true bread, Jesus, is incomparably superior.

Confused over Jesus' spiritual language
Eating his flesh and drinking his blood was not intended literally. It was a question of abiding in him. The same kind of life as Jesus possesses he shares with those who identify with him.

Their unbelief was understandable. They needed a new dimension, a new relationship with Jesus to dispel it. There is still the same need today.

JOHN 6:44
The drawing of the Father

No one comes to Christ unless he is drawn. What does this mean? Why is it necessary?

Several influences are at work on mankind
Man's environment exerts a pull. There is the urge to conform. Man's sin provides a bias away from God. There is need of a higher magnetism to pull the other way.

The Father draws in numerous ways
He sent the Son to be a powerful draw. That drawing is seen

most vividly in the cross (cf. Jn. 12:32). He draws through the Spirit and through men of God, even sometimes through circumstances.

The drawing must be distinguished from compulsion
The drawing is a gentle action which persuades, not a violent action that intimidates. The Father woos rather than frightens.

Some may feel this contravenes man's independence. But the drawing of love respects our freedom. We may never know why we yielded to its magnetism.

JOHN 6:60–65
Grumbling disciples

The disciples were no better than the Jews. Those closest to Jesus were as baffled as the rest. Spiritual truth has always caused difficulties.

The stumbling block
The idea of eating the flesh of Jesus was repugnant to them. They failed to penetrate its truth. But Jesus is sensitive to the difficulty and proceeds to explain.

The ascension to heaven
Jesus uses the title Son of Man in speaking of this. When they saw him ascend they would understand.

The gift of the Spirit
Jesus distinguishes between the Spirit and the flesh. His sayings must be understood in a spiritual sense. They were to learn this later.

The cloud on the horizon
The first hint of betrayal. Not all would understand, for one

would betray. Jesus makes clear that understanding depends on the gracious act of God. There is mystery why it never dawned on Judas.

It is well to vocalise difficulties, for otherwise they may never be illuminated. There are answers we may not have recognised.

JOHN 6:66–71
Differing reactions to Jesus

The moment of decision comes to everyone. What do we really think of him? This section illustrates three different reactions

Many left him

His teaching about himself was too difficult. Many were prepared to follow as long as it did not make any demands. But to regard Jesus as the sole way to God was too much.

Peter confesses him

The twelve are challenged. Peter answers for them. He recognises the uniqueness of Jesus. He alone had promised eternal life. Moreover, they had come to see in Jesus the Holy One of God. There was something about him that made them believe.

Judas was to betray him

Jesus actually calls him a devil. It was only later that the disciples learned the identity of the betrayer. How could a man turn so rapidly against him? It is baffling, but it carries a serious warning.

There are many other possible reactions. But Peter and the others who saw him as the Holy One were those who received the eternal life which Jesus gives.

JOHN 7:1–10
Conflict within the family

This section throws light on Jesus and his brothers. It also shows that family advice must at times be overridden. The plan of God was more important than human suggestions.

A critical situation

The Jews were seeking to kill Jesus in Judea. He decided to work in Galilee. The feast of Tabernacles was approaching. The question was, Should he go to the feast?

Some unbelieving advice

Jesus did not lack advice from his family. Their idea was for Jesus to reveal himself and do works in Jerusalem. The suggestion echoed one of the temptations in appealing to the spectacular. They failed to understand his mission.

A penetrating answer

There is a right time for everything. For Jesus it was 'not yet' (cf. verse 30). His destiny was in God's hands. The action advised by the brothers would precipitate a crisis too soon. The world's hatred is only directed towards those who challenge its evil motives.

That Jesus went up later did not contradict his statement. The contrast was between a public and private appearance.

JOHN 7:7
The alliance between hate and evil

Jesus lived and worked in an adverse environment. The world hated him and he explains why.

The world's works are evil

This seems a drastic assessment. God created the world and called it good. But Jesus speaks of the world of men. All who go against God's purpose are evil. Is this too harsh a judgment?

Jesus witnesses against the world

There was bound to be a clash. His teaching always challenged. Jesus condemned falsehood, covetousness, love of money, misunderstandings of the real purpose of the law.

But he also challenged by his personal lifestyle. The fact that no one could fault him aroused intense hatred. He was too uncomfortable to have around.

Evil finds more use for hate than for love. We should examine carefully our hates.

JOHN 7:11–13
Speculations

Although he went privately, Jesus was the subject of conversation in Jerusalem. Questions and rumours were flying around.

'Where is he?'

The absence of the name shows that he was much talked about, but was treated with contempt. This was no genuine enquiry but a murder search.

'He is a good man'

Some had heard good reports of Jesus. News of his teaching and his works had spread. This reflects some popular support, but was he no more than this?

'He leads people astray'

The same person but a wholly different assessment. We are not told on what grounds they judged. But their opinions were wholly baseless. He is the one person who never misleads.

The speculation was hushed because of the threat of the Jews. There was some concern for Jesus. But they mostly missed the point.

JOHN 7:14–18
The basis of true learning

The focus is on Jesus the teacher. The Jews were used to rabbis' teaching. But Jesus' style and content was unique.

Teaching that astonished

Later it was his style that struck his hearers (verse 46). But here it is his lack of official instruction. He was 'uncertificated', a mere amateur. He had not gone through the system.

Teaching from a higher source

The teaching was from God who had sent him. The authority behind the teaching was all important. But authority is something which requires an inner response.

Man loves systems and an authority structure. But Jesus teaches an authority of the heart.

JOHN 7:19–24
Judging with right judgment

*They misunderstood Jesus' words and
criticised his works. Their judgment was
faulty as Jesus shows.*

He charged them with breaking the law
Moses had given the law, but no one wholly kept it. Their
plot to kill Jesus was against the law. Jesus ignores their jibe
about a demon.

He compares healing with circumcision
Jesus points to an inconsistency here. Was circumcision
more important than a man's wholeness? The distinction
they were drawing shows their biased judgment.

He rejects judgment by appearances
Many snap judgments are without basis because first im-
pressions have been mistaken for truth. They had not
weighed up their priorities. Legalism has no room for this.

*Right judgment requires a right basis. Their
estimate of Jesus was wrong. Are we sure our
estimate is right, so that our judgments about
him will be right?*

JOHN 7:25–31
Perplexity over Jesus

*Jesus has always proved to be an enigma to
many. The Jerusalem people voice some of
their problems.*

Perplexity over their ruler's attitude
Jesus had become a political issue. The plot to kill him was

well known. But nothing was being done. It was a subject of debate. What was the hitch? Perhaps they were ignorant of the identity of Jesus!

Perplexity over the origin of Jesus

'We know where he comes from' reflects some contempt for his humble origins. He did not fit the expected pattern. But Jesus points out that they did not really know his origin. He had come from the one who sent him, that is the Father . . .

Perplexity over his signs

Some thought that the Christ would do not more than Jesus was doing. This kind of questioning led to faith. Some perplexity is productive.

We may ask questions, but we must be prepared for a spiritual answer. If perplexity remains it will be because we have not listened to Jesus' own claims.

JOHN 7:32–36
Mutterings about Jesus

The religious authorities decide to take action. To them Jesus was a threat. This section shows Jesus facing arrest. How did he react?

Jesus warned that the time was short

His life will last only a little longer. The immediate threat will not succeed. He implies that his hearers still have time to respond.

Jesus would be sought and not found

How enigmatic! He must have been thinking of the time after his death. The opportunity is now, but they would leave it too late.

Jesus was going where they could not go

It is not surprising they could not understand. He was going to the Father, but such a concept was beyond them. They thought in terms of the Dispersion, wholly missing the point.

Here is another case of missing spiritual reality by an over-literal approach. We should be warned of the danger, lest we leave our quest until it is too late.

JOHN 7:37–39
The Spirit like living water

At the feast of Tabernacles there was a water ceremonial. Jesus uses it to illustrate some important teaching.

Jesus quenches the believer's thirst
- (a) This assumes a recognition of need. Physical thirst is a fearful experience. But spiritual thirst is often ignored. Why?
- (b) It assumes a relationship with Jesus. Coming to him involves trusting in him and commitment to him.
- (c) It assumes a participation in his life. The believer can draw refreshment from him. Only those who have experienced this can appreciate it.

The believer can bring its benefits to others
- (a) Spiritual supplies flow from committed people. The refreshment is Christ's but the channels are God's people.
- (b) The supplies are unrestricted. The living waters come in rivers, not in trickles.

The metaphorical language is explained

John adds a note which evidently sprang from his own

experience. The 'water' was the Spirit. He realised that it came only after Jesus was glorified. He was presumably thinking of the pouring out of the Spirit at Pentecost.

The subsequent experience of the church abundantly illustrates this truth when the Spirit came to dwell within believers. What kind of flow is there from us?

JOHN 7:40–52
Various reactions to Jesus

The life of Jesus illustrates what has been happening ever since. He continues to evoke different responses. Those in this passage are representative.

The prophet
Not just any prophet, but the special one expected (Deut. 18:18). Some recognised the character of his teaching. The authorities take up the 'prophet' image, but reject it (verse 52).

The Christ
Those holding this are probably those from verse 31. This opinion raised problems. Messiah would come from Bethlehem, whereas Jesus was from Galilee. The objection was invalid since both were true of Jesus.

An incomparable teacher
The officials who came to arrest Jesus were captured by his words. We may reflect on how eloquent Jesus must have been to deflect them from their purpose.

A deceiver
The religious authorities talked about people being led astray. Only those well taught in the law were capable in their eyes of forming a judgment. Nicodemus points out

that the rulers' knowledge was not first hand. They were judging without hearing. This was against their own law.

When faced with Jesus it is impossible to be neutral. There is no room for 'don't knows'.

JOHN 7:40
The prophet

God had spoken through the prophets. They exercised a powerful influence on Israel's history. In one sense Jesus was the prophet par excellence.

He was a prophet because he declared God's word
The prophets' message was 'Thus says the Lord'. Jesus spoke from God.

He was a prophet by virtue of his nature
He had access to the mind of God. He was in the bosom of the Father.

He performed prophetic acts
His signs were acted parables in the style of the prophets.

Theologians have seen Jesus as prophet, priest and king. But the significance of the first is often forgotten. Jesus the prophet should command our attention.

JOHN 7:45, 46
An unexpected testimony

*The arresters were arrested by words. Their
testimony was given to an adverse audience.*

The audience
The bosses issued a challenge, 'Why didn't you bring him?'
The officers had failed in their duty. Some adequate explanation was demanded. The rulers wanted swift action,
not delay.

The witnesses
If the rulers were surprised by Jesus' absence, they were
more so at the reason given. The officers had been overcome by the teaching of Jesus. They must have known they
would incur the wrath of their masters, but this adds to the
powerful character of their testimony.
  (a) They were unbiased witnesses.
  (b) They had heard for themselves.
  (c) They had recognised the unique authority of Jesus.
  (d) They realised that what he said was more impressive
      than the wisdom of their superiors, among whom
      were the leading teachers of the people.

*Testimony from such a source and in such
circumstances is doubly significant. No one
else has ever taught like Jesus.*

JOHN 7:48
Class prejudice and Jesus Christ

The authorities are set against the crowd, the rulers against the people. Class divisions have often been a barrier in the reception of the gospel.

Have any of the authorities believed?
The question implies a negative answer. It also implies a superiority complex among the rulers and the Pharisees. They were on a different level in power and knowledge. They had a contempt for the common people. This attitude is still not uncommon.

But this crowd are accursed
There is a fallacy here. It assumes only the privileged and educated can discern God's way. The common crowd are bound to go astray. The Pharisees did little to remove the curse of ignorance. Its existence enhanced their superiority.

Class prejudice of any kind is a stumbling block to the gospel. We need to analyse our attitudes to discover whether any of this prejudice lurks in our minds.

JOHN 8:1–11 (+ 7:53)
The woman caught in adultery

[This section was almost certainly not originally
a part of this gospel]

*Jesus never condoned adultery, but he shows
great sympathy for the woman. It is a study in
human attitudes.*

The plot
The scribes and Pharisees caught the woman in the act.
Their concern was to apply the law of Moses. Their desire
for morality was laudable, but it was a trap. The question
'What do you say about her?' is personal.

The response
Jesus did not even look up at the accusers or the woman. He
spared her feelings. What he wrote is unimportant. Let the
sinless one cast the first stone was devastating. It was an
appeal to their consciences.

The sequel
As the accusers withdrew one by one, Jesus at last talks to
the woman. No one was left to condemn except Jesus, who
refuses to do so. Yet he issues a challenge which she could
hardly forget. She was certainly given no licence to
continue a life of sin.

*Jesus' approach shows the value of
tenderness. He placed the woman's welfare
above a legalistic interpretation of the law. He
showed that no one is entirely free from
condemnation under the law.*

JOHN 8:12
The Light of the world

*This claim from anyone else would be
arrogant. But for Jesus it has the ring of truth.*

It reveals much about Jesus himself
John has introduced the Light theme in 1:7–9 and here he
gives Jesus' own claim.
- (a) Light is necessary to life in the physical world. The
  same is true of the spiritual.
- (b) Light here is exclusive.
  It is highly personal. 'I am.'
  It is universal. 'The' Light of the 'world'.
This claim to uniqueness has often been challenged
  but never disproved.

It reveals much about man
It implies that apart from Christ all is darkness. This is an
unpalatable doctrine. Yet with all his achievements man
has not been able to escape from his own moral darkness.
There are some lesser lights, some flashes of revelation.
But with Christ the darkness was overcome.

It offers a new possibility
The new way of life is called 'the light of life'. It banishes
darkness and substitutes illumination. Christ sheds light on
every moral decision. Those believing in him are children
of light.

Why grope in the dark when light is available?

JOHN 8:13–20
The Pharisees object to Jesus

Here is a dialogue consisting of an objection,
an explanation and a perplexing question. It
teaches much about Jesus' view of his mission.

The objection
(a) 'You witness to yourself.' Jesus would agree that
self-testimony is suspect (cf. 5:31). But Light does
not need authenticating. Jesus claims to be different.
(b) 'Your witness is not true.' This was a value judgment. Truth was being judged by the wrong
standard.
What they meant was that they did not agree with it.

The explanation
Jesus rejects their assessment on the following grounds:
(a) *He knew his origin and destiny*. Their problem was
that they misunderstood both.
(b) *Their judgment was inadequate*. It was according to
flesh. They were applying their own criteria.
(c) *His witness was supported by the Father*. The law
required a double witness.

The perplexity
'Where is your Father?' They had not recognised that Jesus
was the Son of God. They also failed to know God as
Father. These aspects are complementary. Have a right
view of Jesus and a right view of God will follow.

Jesus still bears witness and his witness is true.
The tragedy is that people still object and miss
the truth.

JOHN 8:21–25
A warning and a challenge

A solemn warning
'You will die in your sins.' This was most disturbing. But what had it to do with Jesus going away? It seems to mean they will not go where he is because of this condemnation.

A flippant reaction
The Jews attempt to deflect the challenge. Sidetracking is the frequent reaction to the direct warnings of the gospel.

A striking contrast
Jesus distinguishes his position from theirs. Below/above; this world/not this world. The cleavage cannot be ignored. Many see Jesus only in terms of their own existence. We cannot judge him simply from below. The one requirement was faith in him.

An imposing question
'Who are you?' It was no doubt asked here with scorn. But there can be no more important question than this. Jesus' answer probably means – I am what I have been saying all along. But it could refer to the beginning of creation or the beginning of Jesus' ministry.

The question of Jesus' identity needs to be posed with a serious intent if the right answer is to be gained.

JOHN 8:25–30
Jesus and the Father working together

Jesus often returns to this theme. He regarded it as of utmost importance to show that his mission was fully supported by the Father.

Jesus declares what the Father has revealed

The truth of the words depends on the truth of the person. But they did not understand. They had not grasped that the sender was the Father.

Jesus predicts the effect of the crucifixion

The up-lifting of the Son of Man would bring greater knowledge. But did it? If we take up-lifting to mean exaltation as well as a reference to crucifixion, it becomes clear. Many recognised that God exalted Jesus.

Jesus affirms that he always pleases the Father

He claims no authority of his own. This identity with the Father tells much about the person of Jesus. It puts him on an equal footing with God.

Many believed then and multitudes have believed since. Do these stupendous claims lead us to faith?

JOHN 8:31–38
The way to freedom

To follow Jesus is the path to freedom. What he says here is relevant for all in bondage.

A promise to disciples
What is a disciple? One who continues in Christ's word. Such a person will experience freedom through the truth. The implication is that true freedom comes no other way.

A problem for those who think they are free
The Jews disliked the idea: 'Abraham's children are already free'. But this was a hollow claim. They were in political and spiritual bondage.

An exposition of true freedom
Jesus speaks of the slavery of sin. But the Son can give real freedom, i.e. of a different kind from what the Jews thought they already possessed. Their plot to kill him did not reflect their claim to freedom. Jesus again contrasts his aims with theirs.

There are still many views about freedom, but Jesus still claims an exclusive right to give it.

JOHN 8:36
The nature of freedom

To be made free implies a previous lack of freedom. What relevance have Jesus' words for our modern world?

False ideas of freedom
These words were uttered against a background of false notions. Today these abound. Man generally thinks he is free to do as he wishes.

False freedom is really bondage

Man is now in the grip of a mechanised and electronic age. The tyranny of ideologies produces widespread fear in the name of freedom. Basically sin still enslaves.

True freedom is linked with truth

Verse 32 makes this clear. But freedom is not a licence to believe what one chooses. True freedom admits the authority of God's teaching. It involves a freedom to submit.

True freedom involves a new bondage

This is a paradox. Paul called himself a bondslave of Christ. True freedom involves a yoke of service (cf. Mt. 11:29). Yet Jesus calls this real freedom. The Christian does as he likes, but he likes to please his Lord.

Have we really been emancipated through Christ? Freedom comes by way of submission.

JOHN 8:39–47
Spiritual genealogy

Origins are important. But human descent is no guarantee of spiritual lineage. Here Jesus raises some important questions.

Descent from Abraham

Every Jew was proud of descent from the patriarch. But what did it involve? Actions speak louder than words, and their actions were aimed to kill God's messenger.

Descent from God

The Jews next claimed God as Father. But again their attitude falsified the claim. They did not love the one who came from the Father. They had no desire to hear the message of Jesus.

Descent from the devil

Jesus shocks his hearers by revealing the true position. They were doing the devil's work. He murders and he lies. They were aligned with one whose nature was to distort. Their unwillingness to listen to Jesus means they are not of God.

> *Only those who believe in Jesus can claim descent as children of God. Our pedigree counts for nothing in this respect.*

JOHN 8:48–50
Jesus under a verbal attack

> *Slander is always a bad weapon. It is particularly so when directed against Jesus, the most perfect person who ever lived.*

Jesus is slandered with baseless allegations

The Jews give up reasoned argument and resort to false statements. 'Samaritan' and 'possessing a demon' were terms of contempt. But note how Jesus answers them.

Jesus rose above such allegations

He ignores the Samaritan jibe. He refutes the demon charge. They must have known the hollowness of the charge.

Jesus appeals to a higher mode of assessment

He honours the Father. They dishonour him. The Father will be the arbitrator over who is right. His purpose is to glorify the Son.

> *Will men never learn the folly of slandering Jesus? His Father will have the last word.*

JOHN 8:51–59
The overcomer of death

The promise of deliverance from death
Death is the great enemy (cf. Heb. 2:14, 15). To be delivered from it would be a real boon. But the Jews ignored this remarkable offer. They simply questioned his right to make it.

The problem about the promise
Abraham and the prophets all died. Not even they claimed power over death. The Jews thought Jesus must be crazy to do so.

The support for the promise
Jesus again appeals to the Father. He claims personal knowledge of him. He claims to keep his word. He even claims to have existed before Abraham.

How ironical that those who rejected the offer of escape from death sought to inflict death on the one who made it! How perverse can men get?

JOHN 8:54–59
Christ and Abraham

Abraham is one of the links between the Old Testament and the New Testament. His relation to Christ is therefore of some importance.

A challenge to Jesus
'Who do you claim to be?' Jesus shows he is Son of God. He claims identity with the Father's purpose. He keeps the Father's word.

A comparison with Abraham

They asked, 'Are you greater than Abraham?' He pointed out:

(a) Abraham rejoiced to see Jesus' day. No details are given about when this was. Perhaps on mount Moriah.

(b) Jesus was before Abraham. 'Before Abraham was I am' claims superiority to Abraham. It is a claim to be God.

The sons of Abraham thought the claims were scandalous. He was fit only to be stoned. But many others were to discover the truth that these Jews had missed.

JOHN 9:1–12
A blind man healed

Healing of physical blindness is here linked with spiritual healing. Jesus was always concerned about the whole person.

The strange question

The disciples assumed that blindness was the result of sin, either the man's own or his parents. The former is surely impossible before birth, but the latter might be supported from Exod. 20:5.

The penetrating answer

Jesus rejects both explanations and gives his own. The immediate purpose was to show God's glory. This is a practical rather than a theoretical approach. There was a necessity for Jesus to do God's work while it was opportune. In other words, this was the priority. Jesus the Light was about to bring light to the man.

The practical method

Clay, spittle and Siloam water were the means. The touch

of Jesus was reassuring to the man who could not see. The immediate action and healing revealed real faith on the man's part.

The resultant curiosity
The sensational healing causes different explanations. Some went as far as arguing for a different man. Others were wanting to know who healed him. Curiosity in this case was understandable, but useless unless it led to Jesus.

Modern miraculous healings can equally result in scepticism or curiosity. But some at least have met with Jesus through signs.

JOHN 9:3
Human suffering

Why suffering is a perpetual problem, especially for those who suffer. What light does this incident throw on Jesus' answer to the problem?

Jesus rejects speculative solutions
Although it may be true that God does not desire suffering, it is harsh to charge the sufferer with sin. It is equally unhelpful to charge the parents with sin, although some suffering is undoubtedly inherited.

Jesus suggests looking beyond the causes
Many have found comfort in the fact that God has been glorified through their suffering. He does not always heal, although in this case he did. Do the words suggest that God's works are more important than the suffering?

This is a profound problem. The Christian must seek to alleviate suffering as far as possible. But the main message is one of triumph over it.

JOHN 9:13–23
The Pharisees investigate: the first encounter

Here is another case of differing religious priorities. Jesus was concerned about the man. The Pharisees were concerned about the sabbath.

The Pharisees investigate
They questioned about the healing, but were more concerned about the sabbath. They show no joy that the man can now see.

The Pharisees disagree
Some said Jesus was not of God; others that a sinner could not do such signs. Both deductions were based on the same evidence.

The healed man's testimony
He was more penetrating. He saw Jesus as a prophet. His insight was more than the Pharisees. Sometimes learning obliterates rather than illuminates.

The investigators' disbelief
Faced with a seeing man, scepticism actually denied the original blindness. But the parents do not support such a view. Through fear they refer back to the son. Their fear implies that they thought Jesus was the Christ.

Even educated people are often incapable of rightly assessing the evidence. Any excuse is better than admitting that God is at work.

JOHN 9:24–34
The Pharisees investigate: the second encounter

This sequel shows a man arguing from experience against prejudice. There is a ring of certainty about what he says.

The entanglement of prejudice
They were tied to the conviction that Jesus was a sinner. Since that was not negotiable, the healed man must glorify God, and virtually deny Jesus' miracle. Did they expect this line of argument to succeed?

The affirmation of experience
He admits to ignorance of Jesus' status, but he knows about Jesus' deeds. 'Though I was blind, now I see.'

The anger of bigotry
Where arguments fail use of slander was their philosophy. 'We are Moses' disciples' reflects their over-confidence. Note the arrogant 'We know' of verses 24, 29.

The challenge of faith
The man marvelled at their lack of knowledge about his healer, in spite of their claims to know about Moses. He uses their type of argument: 'We know' (verse 31). The uniqueness of the healing points to God working through the healer.

The exasperation of privilege
'Would you teach us?' This reversal of roles was intolerable. It must not be allowed. They cast him out.

Can learned teachers ever learn from the simple-minded? History shows that personal experience of Christ is always more powerful than theoretical opinions.

JOHN 9:25
Christian certainty

*Absolute certainty is possible for those who
have experienced an encounter with Christ.
One thing I know.*

Based on experience
He knew he was born blind. He knew clay mixed with
spittle had been applied. He knew he had been to Siloam.
He knew he could now see. None of this could be disputed.
Similarly the spiritually sighted know without doubt.

Based on knowledge
This was severely limited. Indeed he claims to know only
one thing. However limited, he would allow no sidetracking of it. He stood by what he knew. Here is a lesson in
Christian apologetics.

Based on gratitude
His understanding of Jesus was restricted, but he was
grateful for the healing he had received. He springs to
Jesus' defence. 'If this man were not from God he could do
nothing' (verse 33).

*The Christian church spreads through
personal testimony. Christians who have no
skill in argument can always speak of their
experience.*

JOHN 9:35–38
The growth of understanding

There is always room for growing in knowledge of Christ. We cannot rest on our initial experience.

Jesus sought him out
This shows Jesus' concern for the spiritual condition of the man. The challenge was direct – 'Do you believe in the Son of Man?' This is a challenge to personal faith.

Jesus introduces himself
This was a face to face encounter. The healed man looks on his healer. He at once calls him Lord and worships him. See how rapid is the development of faith!

This man was ready for growth. Are we satisfied with our first encounter with Jesus or do we thirst for more knowledge?

JOHN 9:39–41
The purpose of Christ's coming

The specific healing is turned into a general statement of the purpose of the incarnation in terms of light.

He came to judge
This cannot be considered the main aim. But it was unavoidable. Judgment is the obverse side of salvation. Christ's coming involves a double effect.

He came to give sight
The seeing is spiritual sight rather than physical. This reflects the 'light of the world' saying in 8:12.

He came to show people their blindness

Many think they see. But their standards are wrong. Jesus confronts the Pharisees who will not admit their blindness and shows them to be guilty on that account.

Jesus has always had a twofold effect on people. Some receive the glorious light he came to give; others are content to remain in a state of moral and spiritual blindness.

JOHN 10:1–6
The allegory of the shepherd

Pictorial language is valuable for presenting spiritual truths. Generally Jesus used parables. But here he uses the more extended form of allegory.

The sheepfold

In the Old Testament God is seen as the Shepherd of Israel. Jewish hearers would at once recognise this. In the New Testament the church is the fold.

The door

Each fold had one acknowledged way of entry. This is equally so of the messianic kingdom. Jesus is about to introduce himself as the door (verse 7).

The false shepherd

Anyone using another method of entry is false. The climbing in represents any alternative means. Here the points made are robbery and strangeness. The sheep do not naturally follow. Force is needed.

The true shepherd

He has a rightful entry. He leads his sheep. He calls them by name. The emphasis falls on relationship. The following is natural, because the shepherd has their interest at heart.

In this way Jesus leads his hearers to think about himself. It is a valuable example for all communicators of the gospel. He whetted their appetite for more understanding.

JOHN 10:4, 27
Knowing the voice of Jesus

There is something reassuring for the sheep about the shepherd's voice. It is considerably more so for the people of God.

The sheep know the shepherd's voice
This happens through experience. The constant sound of the voice impresses itself on the sheep. We must listen carefully to catch the distinctive sounds of the good shepherd's voice.

The sheep follow the voice they know
Knowing is not enough. When the shepherd calls, the sheep follow. They must have full confidence in the voice. They will not follow strangers. We should know how Jesus communicates so that we keep within his purposes.

Keep within the sound of his voice for the sake of security and right direction. Perhaps we need more often to tune in to what he is saying.

JOHN 10:7–10
I am the door

*Here Jesus applies one part of the allegory.
This illustrates his progressive method of
teaching.*

Jesus claims a unique position
He is the sole way to salvation. There is no suggestion
of him being one among others. The article (*the* door)
emphasises this.

Jesus rejects all other shepherds
This exclusiveness cannot be avoided. By comparison with
Christ other methods of salvation are illegitimate – 'thieves
and robbers' is strong language. Jesus sees alternative
salvation as destructive.

Jesus offers abundant life
The end product in salvation is a better life. This must be
understood spiritually. The 'life' theme is strong in John. It
is linked with eternal life.

*The switch from door to life may seem
strange, but the idea of entrance into life is
highly significant. Do we regard Jesus'
exclusive claims as justified?*

JOHN 10:10
Life more abundant

Life is a big word. Some use it as equivalent to fate (life has been hard on me). Others as standing for enjoyment (I want to see life). But the Christian view is entirely different.

Life was the purpose of Christ's coming
To come to give life was a costly business. It involved the cross. The life he came to give is like his own. He demonstrates the new quality of life he gives.

Life could not be given by any others
The best of them are compared to thieves. They had no desire to enhance the life of the flock. Their approach was negative and destructive. Many benefits do come from other sources, but not life.

Life was intended to be abundant
God never gives stintingly. He always gives his best. He gave his son. Life should be overflowing, infectious, triumphant.

Life more abundant is everlasting
There can be no end to it. When Jesus gives life it is destined to last. This is no temporary euphoria. Fully abundant life cannot be experienced on earth. We need a more perfect environment for its fullest expression.

It must be admitted that many Christians do not live with such exuberant life. Are we too easily satisfied?

JOHN 10:11–18
The good shepherd

Here is another great 'I am' saying. This claim is implied in the preceding passage. The true shepherd and the door prepare for the good shepherd.

His character

Jesus was more than a good man. He was the supreme example of goodness. Moreover as a shepherd he was good because he cared for the flock. Every flock needs the right kind of shepherd.

His intervention

He lays down his life. Jesus looks ahead towards the cross. How could his hearers have understood? But we who look back on events can grasp what he has done on our behalf. The good shepherd protects his sheep from the wolf.

His knowledge

He knows his sheep and they know him. This deep personal relationship between shepherd and sheep is significant. Such a personal relationship is central to Christian faith. The pattern for such knowledge is no less than the Father's knowledge of the son.

His vision

He speaks of other folds within the one flock. He looks beyond the narrow confines of Judaism to a universal flock. His shepherd heart goes out to them.

Three times in this passage Jesus speaks of the shepherd laying down his life. This was the most important thing he ever did.

JOHN 10:14–16
The shepherd and his sheep

*In the rural communities of Palestine the
shepherd illustration would be particularly
meaningful. The analogy has its weakness in
that people are more responsible than sheep.
But it is highly suggestive.*

Jesus is the right kind of shepherd
He is genuinely interested in his sheep. There is no sham.
His essential goodness ensures the utmost care for his
people.

Jesus made the supreme sacrifice for his sheep
The cross stands at the centre of the Christian faith. Here is
one explanation of it – an act on behalf of others. The laying
down of life was voluntary (see verse 18).

Jesus develops a special relationship with his sheep
  (a) He knows them and they know him.
  (b) He possesses his sheep. 'I know my own.'
  (c) He yearns over his sheep.
  (d) He unites his sheep into one flock.

*When Christians feel isolated it is a great
encouragement to remember that the shepherd
knows and cares.*

JOHN 10:17, 18
The death of Christ

*This gospel gives many insights into the
meaning of the death of Christ. Here we see
that event as by no means unexpected.*

It arises from the Father's love
It is difficult to reconcile the cross with God's love. But
Jesus sees a close connection. If we approach the cross
through the love of God it becomes transformed.

It is a voluntary act
In the light of subsequent events this is perplexing. Did not
wicked men forcefully crucify him? In what sense did Jesus
lay down his life? Perhaps Gethsemane is the answer. He
accepted God's will. He permitted the arrest.

It was followed by resurrected life
Jesus looks ahead to the resurrection. The early church
soon learned that death must be linked to resurrection.

*He could have held on to his life, but he gave
it. The giving of it up was a charge he had
received from his Father.*

JOHN 10:19–21
Divided opinion about Jesus

*We have met it before. We are reminded again
that there will always be supporters and
opposers of Jesus.*

Why listen to him?
It is easy to classify as demon possessed someone who
challenges us too pointedly. It means we can ignore what he
says. But such an approach needs justification. Anyone

regarding Jesus as demon possessed is calling good evil. His values are totally wrong.

Why not listen to him?
Some looked harder at the evidence. Two facts stood out. He talked in a marvellous way. And he opened blind people's eyes. An impartial approach should rule out the demon charge. It didn't make sense. Such an attitude prepares the way for a further quest.

Those who have written him off and refused to listen to him do so at their peril.

JOHN 10:22–30
The shepherd speaks again

It was winter in Jerusalem. Jesus was accosted by those wanting an unambiguous statement from him. In reply he returns to the shepherd theme.

The Father's works and the shepherd's sheep
Jesus claims that his works are the Father's works. The works spoke volumes about the Son. But those who saw them did not believe. They were outside the flock.

The shepherd's sheep in the shepherd's hand
They hear his voice and follow. They receive eternal life. They have complete security. No harm can come to them.

The shepherd's hand is the Father's hand
No distinction is made between them. Security is doubled by the complete identity between the purpose of Father and Son. 'I and my Father are one.'

There is mystery here. Father and Son are distinct, yet one. Jesus never acts contrary to the will of the Father.

JOHN 10:28, 29
No snatching away

These verses have led to the doctrine of the final preservation of the saints. They speak of certain security.

Christ does not give tentatively
Eternal life would not be eternal if it could be lost. God's purposes cannot be thwarted when he has given such a priceless gift.

He does not permit snatching
The idea of believers being in Christ's hands is a comforting thought. Any attack on them must overcome formidable fortifications. But Christ promises this will prove impossible.

His hold on his people is reinforced by the Father
This is a kind of second line of defence. The Godhead is intent on preserving the hard won trophies of grace.

We may have formidable enemies, but we have an even more formidable protection. The 'no snatching' promise is the basis of complete security.

JOHN 10:31–39
Was Jesus blaspheming?

The charge of blasphemy is serious. Why was it made? Follow the steps by which truth can be so completely distorted.

Jesus questions his attackers
He challenges them to state the charge against him. The stones were in their hands. Why this fury?

The Jews allege blasphemy

'Being a man, you call yourself God.' This was most perceptive, because it was true. But on the interpretation of the facts there was grave difference. He alone was both. They saw him as a man, but could not credit that he could be God.

Jesus vindicates his claim to deity

He appeals to the Old Testament. The argument seems strange to us, but his hearers would get the point. He was consecrated and sent by the Father. He appeals also to his works and sees them as a basis for faith.

No amount of explanation will change the attitude of those intent on ridding themselves of Jesus. He escaped from them on this occasion for his time had not come.

JOHN 10:40–42
Some response beyond the Jordan

We have here a summary of a brief visit. Most of John's gospel shows Jesus in Jerusalem. But see what happened in Perea.

The place had historic connections

It was where John the Baptist had baptised. It had seen multitudes repenting as a result of the fiery preaching. It had witnessed the baptism of Jesus and John's testimony to him as the Lamb of God. It was there that a heavenly voice had spoken.

The people had learned from those connections

They had had time to test out John's words about Jesus. Their verdict was that everything was true. They did the obvious thing and believed.

JOHN 11:1–16
The crisis over Lazarus

*Here is Jesus confronted with death. The
raising to life was the most stupendous of
miraculous events. It becomes viable in the
light of Christ's own resurrection.*

Crisis at Bethany
It was a home known to Jesus and much used by him. It was
an oasis in a hostile world. Mary had anointed the feet of
Jesus. Martha had served him. Now Lazarus was ill. They
sent to Jesus for help.

Jesus' reaction to the crisis
He declares the sickness is (a) not unto death, (b) for God's
glory. Although Lazarus died he lived again and God was
glorified in the event. But why did Jesus delay?

The disciples' reaction to Jesus' plans
The prospect of going back to Judea daunted them. The
Jews had threatened Jesus. Fear was a powerful deterrent.

Jesus' reaction to the disciples
A twelve hour day offers opportunity for work. For Jesus
the day of his life had not yet ended. No threats could stop
him finishing his task. Moreover he must wake Lazarus
from sleep.

The disciples' reaction to Jesus' statements
Lazarus could surely wake up on his own! When Jesus said
he was dead, Thomas gloomily offers to die with Jesus.
Such heroics took no account of Jesus' power over death.

The disciples' appreciation of the power of Jesus was severely limited. Is ours any better in spite of our knowledge of Jesus' own resurrection? Or do we write the miracle off as impossible?

JOHN 11:5
The friendship of Jesus

We have a brief glimpse into the private life of Jesus. The Bethany home was a special haven for him during his ministry.

The family at Bethany

Martha was an activist as we learn from Lk. 10:38–42. Mary was more contemplative. John says she had anointed the Lord with ointment. Of Lazarus we know nothing. But this incident shows them to have been a close-knit family. The sisters were deeply affected by the loss of Lazarus.

The special friend of the family

Jesus loved them. They are especially privileged in the gospel narrative to have this recorded. Jesus clearly had a special relation with them. The great teacher and miracle worker relaxed in this home.

He desires to share that friendship with others

Later in the gospel Jesus tells his disciples he will call them friends (Jn. 15:15). There is no greater friendship than this – someone who lays down his life for his friends (Jn. 15:13, 14). The tender relationship with the Bethany home is some indication of the meaning of this.

Jesus is the friend of sinners. His friendship involves a deep concern for their welfare.

JOHN 11:15
For your sake

No one ever lived so totally committed to the service of others. These words sum up this self-less purpose.

The circumstances
The death of Lazarus is representative of Jesus' approach to all his activities. He looked at events to discover ways of turning them to a useful purpose.

The delay
This is perhaps the strangest aspect of the whole story. According to verse 6 he stayed two days after hearing that Lazarus was ill. Why? Jesus answers – 'for your sake'. He was even glad not to have been there. The delay was part of the vicarious process.

The sequel
The disciples are not mentioned again in the story. But the words 'for your sake' imply that they witnessed the miracle. Were they stirred by his tears and by his death shattering command? It was probably only after Jesus' own resurrection that they came to understand.

Jesus' actions were designed to serve a long term purpose. This is still true in his dealings with us.

JOHN 11:17–27
Jesus and Martha

*This throws light on a human situation
following a death in the family. It has
relevance in all such situations, particularly
among Christians.*

Martha's mourning over a dead brother
Jews from Jerusalem had come to console. Evidently the
family was well known. But no consolation could compare
with that of Jesus. Martha goes to meet him. In times of
sorrow the best intentioned human sympathy falls short.
Martha's action was doubtless more helpful than Mary's
inaction.

Martha's faith in face of suffering
She believes Jesus could have prevented death. She even
believes that Jesus could do something now. He has only to
ask God and he will do it. She refrains from stating what.

Martha's perplexity over the resurrection
Martha misunderstands Jesus' assurance that Lazarus will
return to life. But it gives her the opportunity to affirm her
belief in the final resurrection. It led also to Jesus' own
affirmation – 'I am the resurrection'.

Martha's developing understanding
She confesses Jesus as Christ and Son of God before the
miracle. It speaks highly of her perception. The miracle
would confirm her faith.

*Faced with crisis of a personal kind, does our
faith grow stronger or does it collapse?*

JOHN 11:21–27
Faith under trial

When faith is under pressure it reveals its true nature. Martha is a good example of a person with faith that develops.

Its strong basis

Her knowledge of Jesus was sufficient to lead to confidence that he could have done something had he been present. It was grounded in a belief that Jesus had a close relationship with God. This was faith in what Jesus could do.

Its severe testing

Why had Jesus delayed to come? She must have known he could have got there earlier. But it had not destroyed what faith there was. It had rather strengthened it. She did not complain about the delay.

Its general challenge

Faced with Jesus' words that Lazarus would rise again, she responds in a general way. She believed in the resurrection at the last day. But what real help was that now? She probably drew some comfort from it as many other mourners have.

Its personal challenge

When Jesus said, 'I am the resurrection and the life' what was she to do? And when he asked, 'Do you believe this?' she was forced to face the issue squarely.

Its clear testimony

Martha makes a profound confession. It no longer concerns what Jesus can do, but who he is. 'The Christ' and 'the Son of God' is comprehensive. That people should believe this was the purpose of this gospel (20:31).

Martha was the prototype of all who would come to faith in Christ.

JOHN 11:25, 26
I am the resurrection

Jesus is making a personal claim. Belief in a coming resurrection was one thing. But such belief needs to become personal faith.

Resurrection leads to life
This gospel says much about life. Jesus came to give life (Jn. 1:4). Frequently the promise of eternal life occurs.

Resurrection comes through faith in Jesus
He twice stresses the need for believing in him. It is in fact the purpose of the gospel to lead people to believe in him. This incident illustrates this (cf. Jn. 11:27 and 20:31).

When we receive Christ, we receive the resurrection. This is the sole means by which we avoid dying in a spiritual sense.

JOHN 11:28–37
Jesus and Mary

We find Jesus dealing with a very different temperament in the case of Mary. The incident shows his sympathetic understanding of her particular needs.

Martha's message for Mary
Martha has found comfort in the presence of Jesus and wants Mary to share it. Mary leaves to go to Jesus and the Jews follow. But why didn't Jesus go to her?

Mary's word to Jesus
Her comment precisely echoes Martha's. But she breaks down and weeps. She lacks the resilience of Martha. But Jesus meets her on her own level.

Jesus' agitation

Why this emotional reaction? Perhaps because of the formal mourning of the Jews and because of the deep sorrow of the sisters. He weeps with those who weep. Some onlookers see it as an evidence of Jesus' love. Others said Jesus could have prevented it. But none said he could raise the dead.

When Jesus saw Mary's tears he also wept. What comfort to know he understands! How often do we so closely identify with the sorrowing?

JOHN 11:35
The tears of the mighty

The raising of Lazarus was an emotional occasion for Jesus. It was to be a type of his own rising from the dead.

Tears of sympathy

Jesus weeps as a friend with those who weep. But he also wept as the master of the situation. The tears showed his human feeling. He could be touched with a feeling for our infirmities (cf. Heb. 4:14).

Tears of sorrow

He knew the bliss into which Lazarus had entered. He also knew the sad state of the earth to which he was about to return. Perhaps Jesus weeps because he knows earth is no match for heaven.

Tears of anguish

He knew the hypocrisy of those around him. He knew the unbelief in men's hearts. These tears were from the same fount which flowed over the sad state of Jerusalem. They came from a deeply troubled mind.

*Those who looked for a triumphant leader
would be astonished at the weeping Messiah.
Some may scoff at a God in tears, but the
sorrowing will rejoice at the sight.*

JOHN 11:38–44
The raising of Lazarus

*Jesus shows his mastery over death. There is
pathos here as he confronts man's last enemy.*

The command of Jesus
The rolling away of the stone was a human action. But the
raising was a divine act. The stone was not included in the
miracle as it was to be at Jesus' resurrection. Martha's
objection was understandable. But Jesus reminds her of his
promise.

The prayer of Jesus
It was thanksgiving for the answer to a prayer already
offered. There was perfect understanding between Father
and Son. The purpose of the miracle was to produce faith.

The miracle of Jesus
The loud voice was so that all the observers could hear it.
The emergence of the dead man bound must have startled
everyone. They needed to be told to unbind him. The
impossible had happened.

*Lazarus had a temporary release from death.
The narrative gives no indication of his
feelings on receiving such a summons. The
story focuses on the immense power of Jesus.*

JOHN 11:40
Seeing the glory of God

*Jesus recognised that miracles would be
windows through which the glory of God
would shine. John brings this out powerfully
in his gospel.*

Seeing comes through faith
God's glory can be seen only through the eye of faith. The
condition is clear – 'if you would believe'.

Seeing will reveal the unexpected
Martha had no idea what was about to happen. The glory of
God has so many manifestations. But those in tune with
Jesus will never miss it. Yet many saw Lazarus come from
the grave but never saw the glory of God.

*The glory of God is often seen most vividly
when all is dark. In times of deepest sorrow
the eye of faith sees traces of that glory.*

JOHN 11:45–53
Reactions to the miracle

*As with all divine signs the reactions differ.
This incident shows that the most powerful
sign is lost on those already determined to
oppose.*

In some faith developed
They had seen what they concluded must be a true work of
God. They were a direct answer to the prayer of Jesus.
They had seen and believed that God had sent him.

In others antagonism developed
The stages are worth observing. The religious rulers

assessed the miracle politically. It was too powerful for them to ignore the possible effect. They were scared of people believing.

In the high priest expediency developed
He considered one should die rather than that all should perish. He little realised that his comment explained the death of Jesus. He was to die for others.

John twice notes that the words were uttered by the high priest that year as if it was important because of his office. He also notes the purpose of Jesus was to gather together the people of God.

None of these people remained unaffected by Jesus. It is impossible simply to ignore him. He challenges us to a decision.

JOHN 11:49–53
Caiaphas

The high priest showed more wisdom than he realised. What he said throws light on the mission of Jesus.

His privileged position
As high priest he represented the people of Israel. He should have recognised the Messiah but he missed his opportunity. His religious opinions were too much dominated by political concerns.

His arrogant attitude
There is an air of superiority about his words 'You know nothing at all'. They were unnecessary as the Pharisees had already suggested some action must be taken against Jesus. All were agreed that he was a threat to them.

His unwitting wisdom

He recognised the principle of substitution. One should die rather all should perish. This was God's principle of salvation. John notes that the high priest was stating a prophecy, which Christians later recognised.

Caiaphas was concerned only for his own nation. But God was concerned about all his scattered children. Jesus died that others might live. See how God uses men's evil designs for his own purpose.

JOHN 11:54–57
A rural retreat

A determined plan to kill Jesus causes a temporary withdrawal. Note how Jesus handles such a situation.

Quietness in Ephraim

It was on the edge of desert. It is thought to have been a few miles north of Jerusalem, although the exact location is unknown. There Jesus was alone with his disciples. John does not divulge what took place. But the quietness was needed before the terrible events of the passion.

Expectation in Jerusalem

Jews from the country were looking for Jesus prior to the feast. They knew of the plot. These were not the people who would naturally go against Jesus, but the threats of the religious rulers were very real.

The contrast here is striking. It shows the quiet before the storm. Jesus would choose his own time to reveal himself. He leaves no doubt that he is in command.

JOHN 12:1–8
Supper time in Bethany

The family had been reunited. The bond with Jesus was strengthened. We might have expected some note on Lazarus' experiences but none is given. Instead we have a supper, just six days before the Passover feast.

Loving care amid gathering clouds
The concern of the family at Bethany for Jesus' needs is in touching contrast to the threats. They refused to be intimidated. Their action furnishes an example for others in times of threats to the people of God.

Special fragrance for a special guest
Whether Mary's action was premeditated or impulsive is not stated. John notes the costliness of the act. It was an expression of deep love that has reached far beyond the bounds of that home. Do we value Jesus as highly as Mary did?

Carping criticism from a dissident disciple
Even the most beautiful acts will attract their critics. The charge of waste may seem quite reasonable in view of the many poor people around. But John comments that Judas was a thief. And Jesus defends the act because of its significance for his coming burial.

Mary's sacrificial act has lived on. The fragrance in the house soon vanished. But the fragrance of her devotion to Jesus has continued to inspire believers through the centuries. We never know the horizons of our acts of love to Jesus.

JOHN 12:9–11
Magnetism and murder

*Once again we are faced with opposing
reactions to Jesus. Some are drawn; others are
repelled. It is mystifying why some people
never see any good in him.*

The attraction of Jesus

Great crowds sought him out. They had heard about the
raising of a dead man. This was clearly sensational. They
wanted to see Jesus and Lazarus. We are not told the
reason for the attraction to Jesus. They no doubt sensed a
powerful divine worker. But many were coming to faith.

The opposition to Jesus

His enemies had already planned to kill Jesus. Now they
extend that to Lazarus. The decision shows how illogical
blind opposition can be. Lazarus has already died once.
What purpose would be served by a plot to kill him?

*We might have expected religious authority to
welcome a mass movement of faith. But their
opposition sprang from envy and fear for their
own position. Men are still opposing the mass
appeal of the gospel.*

JOHN 12:12–19
Entering Jerusalem

*So important was this event seen to be that all
the gospels record it. John puts his own
particular slant on it.*

The acclamation of the crowds

These appear to be Galileans who had come to the feast.
The significance of the palm branches was to represent

triumph. These people seem convinced that Jesus was the Messiah. They probably did not use the word 'Hosanna' with the meaning 'save', but John saw the point of it.

The King of Israel on an ass
Jesus was portraying a very different kind of messiah than most people expected. The lowly animal was fitting for a suffering messiah. John notes the prophecy of Zech. 9:9. Events were not turning out by accident.

The confusion of the Pharisees
To them the shouting crowds around Jesus were alarming. It raised a certain sense of helplessness: 'You can do nothing'. But the fact is they did act and put him on a cross.

Many wanted to acclaim a powerful miracle worker. He might be useful to them. But were any of these people among those who soon after cried 'Crucify'? We do not know. But it is all too easy to be inconsistent.

JOHN 12:20–33
The hour of Jesus

The crucifixion was not an accident. It was planned by God. The 'hour' was the climax of the plan.

The hour of triumph
The entry into Jerusalem looked like a triumph. Yet the ass was incongruous and the various reactions all missed the point. It was intended to be royal, but a royal sacrifice.

The hour of enquiry
The Greeks had a noble quest. It is doubtful whether they understood the significance of the hour. But they were on the right track.

The hour of glory
No one really grasped the nature of the glory. It was not obvious. Only afterwards did the disciples realise the glory of the self-giving of Jesus.

The hour of sacrifice
The corn of wheat explains how dying can be glorious. The greatest glory is the reproduction of the seed. But this required the giving up of life to produce life.

The hour of example
What was true for Jesus also applies to his followers. To keep life his followers must hate it, i.e. hate it as it is lived by the natural man. A higher norm has been introduced.

The hour of anguish
His soul was troubled. These words echo the cry from Gethsemane. A divine voice speaks on Jesus' behalf and the bystanders thought it had thundered.

The hour of judgment
The ruler of this world was about to be cast out. This happened when Jesus died. That event was a judgment on this world and its sin.

The hour of magnetism
At the cross Jesus would draw all men to him. This has always been a paradox. But the cross is a mighty magnet because of the person of Jesus. It speaks a universal language.

That hour in spite of its sorrow was the most glorious hour in human history. From it stemmed the Christian church.

JOHN 12:20–26
The search for Jesus

*The Galilean crowds had heard about a
remarkable sign and had sought him out.
Here some Greek proselytes seek for him.*

The quest
They were serious-minded people who had come to the
feast. They asked someone who knew the answer. Philip
and Andrew were like signposts. They also sought for
someone who was available.

The announcement of Jesus
(a) His hour had come. Several times earlier in the
   gospel there are references to the hour as 'not yet'. It
   is described as an hour of glorification.
(b) The grain must fall. The hearers were meant to see
   Jesus himself as the corn of wheat. Death is needed
   to produce new life. But the grain is reproductive.
   Because Jesus died he produced much fruit in a
   multitude of believers.
(c) The spiritual principle of self-giving applies equally
   to the followers of Jesus. Serving and following Jesus
   involves sacrificial action. Jesus himself would be the
   supreme example of this.

*We are not told whether the Greeks
responded. But we do know that many have
since responded to the teaching of Jesus. Has
the principle of self-giving formed any part of
our present life style?*

JOHN 12:21
The desire to see Jesus

*We know nothing of the Greeks who sought
for Jesus. But their desire is itself worth
pondering.*

Why do people want to see Jesus?
The Greeks may have been motivated by curiosity or
superstitious belief or spiritual hunger. There are many
reasons why people today want to know more about Jesus.

What makes them concentrate on him?
They assume he was sufficiently well-known simply to be
called Jesus. There was no one to compare with him. Many
are fascinated with Jesus but get no further than that.

What help did they get?
They were helped by disciples of Jesus who acted as escorts.
A similar task falls to all whose personal experience of
Jesus equips them to guide others to him.

What was the result of their desire?
They had a conversation with Jesus. They discovered something about his coming death. The result was no doubt
more challenging than they had thought.

*No one can see too much of Jesus. But the
more we see the more we shall understand his
passion and his desire to draw others to him.*

JOHN 12:24, 25
Life-producing death

The New Testament is full of paradoxes. But the greatest is the principle that death is necessary to life.

This is the principle of the natural world
The annual cycle of the dying down of nature in the autumn and the resurrection in the spring is a constant reminder that the new season depends on the death of the old.

This is also the principle of the spiritual world
When applied to human affairs it becomes difficult to accept. It is so contrary to rational thought which is based on self-interest (loving life). But experience shows that self-giving (hating life) is more productive.

Self-giving is costly but highly rewarding. Jesus sets the pattern for his followers.

JOHN 12:27, 28
A prayer of Jesus

The way we pray reveals much of our character. Especially is this so in times of great stress. We are here allowed to listen to a profound prayer of Jesus.

This prayer arose from a time of anguish
The gospels do not often mention the distress of Jesus. But with the approach of the passion, the tension was noticeable. How thankful we should be that Jesus was not shielded from such stress.

This prayer resulted from heart-searching
Here is Jesus having a dialogue with himself. He could have

asked to be saved from the hour but he rejects this. He knew there were more important issues than his own safety. He had come to this hour for a purpose. His request was simple: 'Father, glorify your name'.

This prayer was immediately answered
Only three times did a heavenly voice speak. God answers in different ways, but this warranted a direct answer. To glorify Jesus was God's greatest desire. It was easy to answer because it was directly reflecting God's will.

> *Have we learned the secret of simple prayers that sum up God's purpose? Or are we inclined to persuade God what to do? Every Christian ought to pray the same prayer as Jesus.*

JOHN 12:31, 32
The attraction of Jesus

We are confronted here with two powerful personalities – the ruler of this world and Jesus. The former is cast out and the latter exercises a magnetic drawing power.

Jesus shows his superiority
His enemies put him to death. But they did not realise they were assisting in the defeat of their own ruler. The cross is the historic moment of the devil's defeat.

Jesus emphasises his own attractiveness
The 'I' is emphatic. Such a statement by anyone else would be presumptuous. But on his lips the words are enhanced. It is none other than God's Son who claims such power.

Jesus affirms the drawing power of the cross
The up-lifting is both the act of crucifixion and the exal-

tation which followed it. The winsomeness of his earthly
life was enhanced by the triumph of his death.

Jesus recognises his universal appeal

We should note that he speaks of drawing and not driving.
Although everyone has not been drawn, it is certainly true
that people of all types have been attracted. No class of
people have failed to experience the fascination of Jesus.

The church has not grown because of its .
intrinsic strength or through human effort, but
by the captivating power of Jesus.

JOHN 12:34–36
Groping in the dark

Many are hampered by inadequate
knowledge. They thought they knew about the
Christ. The real problem was the lifting up.
The Jews could not accept a crucified messiah.

The hearers enquire how the Son of Man
can be lifted up?

The cross was unintelligible to those who looked for a
deliverer-messiah. No one could ever conquer that way!

The hearers are urged to walk in the light

This implies that the questioners were in the dark. But
there was still time. Only those who walk in light know
where they are going. After this further invitation, Jesus
hid himself.

Here is another call to faith. Believe in the
light, i.e. in Jesus himself.

JOHN 12:35, 36
Planning life's journey

*The metaphor of walking is often used in the
New Testament for the journey of life. Jesus
here uses it to issue advice and warning.*

The value of daylight
Jesus has already announced himself as the Light. It would
be foolish to travel in darkness if it was possible to travel in
daylight.

The disadvantage of darkness
Where darkness reigns it stands to reason that chaos will
result. Life without knowing where we are going is hazar-
dous. Yet so many neglect to receive the light that Jesus has
provided.

The possibilities of light
Jesus knows his presence with them is limited and uses this
to urge faith. Of course the light will still shine after his
death. But those who believe are promised a new status –
children of light – which means their paths will never be in
the dark.

*There need be no dark patches for the
Christian, since Jesus is a light that never goes
out.*

JOHN 12:37–43
Unbelief and its reasons

*In face of the most remarkable signs people
did not believe. This is most perplexing. John
gives an explanation.*

Signs are not sufficient to produce faith
Even a raising from the dead did not dislodge doubt.
Unbelief is resilient to the most potent evidence.

Unbelief is no new thing
Isaiah found it in his own day as the quote from Isaiah 53
shows. The Old Testament has a trail of unbelief. It is not
surprising that the coming of Jesus made no difference.

Unbelief has a spiritual cause
Another quote from Isaiah 6 raises problems. It looks as if
God had blinded their eyes. What is clear is that unbelief
springs from spiritual blindness. Yet it is still man's own
responsibility that he refuses to believe. Isaiah saw a glory
which his contemporaries did not see.

Some belief is stifled by fear
Even some of the authorities believed. But the cost of
confession was too high. Love of reputation is a powerful
deterrent against siding with Jesus.

*With such a wonderful Saviour, it is sad that
eyes of so many are blinded that they miss the
joy of a new relationship.*

JOHN 12:42, 43
The importance of confession

Secret faith has always appealed to some who lack the courage of their convictions.

What did they do
Some believed but were secretive about it. It is possible for faith about Jesus to develop without anyone knowing about it. But what kind of faith is this?

Why did they do it
John gives two reasons. The first was fear of men. To be disadvantaged in a religious sense meant social ostracism. The claims of Jesus are always clashing with some accepted conventions.

The second is love of men's praise. The followers of Jesus had to forgo this. They knew that faith in Jesus was more valuable than man's estimation.

What was the result of their action?
Did any of them later confess their faith? It is worth observing that Nicodemus started as a secret disciple (cf. Jn. 3:1ff and 7:50ff, and the sequence in 19:39). But lack of confession makes it easier to fall away.

Note the link between confession and faith in Rom. 10:9. Faith in Jesus is too important to be secret.

JOHN 12:44–50
Jesus' last sermon

Here are words which Jesus cries out. He clearly desires them to be heard. They contain important truths about his mission.

Jesus and the believer
Christian faith is more than belief about a person. It is faith in a person who is sent from God. It enables people to see God by seeing Jesus. Jesus' purpose is to cast light into a dark world.

Jesus and the unbeliever
Whoever hears has a responsibility. He must face the challenge. If he rejects he must face the judgment of God. Jesus is not here condemning, for he came to save not to judge. But at the last day his words will be the judge. What we have done about them will be the test.

Jesus and the Father
The words of Jesus have the authority of God. Those who listen to his words must recognise this. Both Father and Son are intent on giving us eternal life.

With such powerful words to challenge us what is our response?

JOHN 13:1–11
The feet washing

Only John relates this. He probably vividly remembered the extraordinary event. The stooping Jesus with towel around him was unforgettable.

The setting
It was just before the Passover feast. Jesus knows what is about to happen. He feels a deep love for his disciples. But he also knows there is treachery in the midst.

The preparation
The removal of the cloak and girding with a towel indicated he was taking on the servant role. This is explained against the background of his eternal mission.

The washing
The menial task of washing feet was undertaken by the master. The conventions of the world would not understand this reversal. But the example was more powerful than words.

The objection
Peter's reaction was understandable and indeed commendable. It spoke of his high regard for Jesus. It also reveals his impudence in dictating to him. Jesus gently points out his ignorance of the symbolism.

The over-reaction
When Peter yields he still adopts a directive approach. 'Wash me all over' was quite unnecessary. Nevertheless Jesus assures him that he will be clean. He will contrast sharply with the betrayer.

Some Christians still observe a feet-washing ceremony. But even where the physical act is not done the significance of humble service to others should be the hallmark of Christianity.

JOHN 13:1
The love of Jesus

*Although Jesus was drawing near to his death,
his concern for his disciples was evident, as
John reminds us.*

He loved his own
They were an unpredictable lot of people. They did not
really appreciate what he had come to do. But with all their
weaknesses he loved them.

He loved them to the end
There is nothing fickle about the love of Jesus. His love is
unchanging. It does not even depend on our love for him. It
is the most wonderful love the world has ever known.

*The apostles came to learn increasingly the
marvellous love of Jesus for them. This is the
spring of all our love for him. He first
loved us.*

JOHN 13:3
Jesus' awareness of his mission

*The events in the life of Jesus are never
recorded as accidents of history. There is a
conviction on the part of this evangelist that
Jesus is conscious of his own destiny.*

Knowledge of the Father's commission
Several times we are told that Jesus claimed to do the will of
him who sent him. Here it is summed up in a comprehensive statement. Everything had been given into his hands.

Knowledge of his origin

He had come from God. He was more than man and he knew it. This awareness gives no support to those who begin with the humanity of Jesus. We cannot understand his mission apart from recognition of his divine origin.

Knowledge of his destination

As he faced the cross his thought was on his approaching return to God. The resurrection and ascension were powerful influences on the closing events of his life.

We shall never fathom the self-awareness of Jesus. In it is bound up the mystery of the incarnation. But we cannot dispense with the mystery.

JOHN 13:12–20
A symbolic act explained

The act needed explanation because it was so contrary to what the disciples expected. It seemed undignified. But it was intended as a symbolic illustration.

The challenge to their understanding

Do you know what I have done to you? Clearly Jesus is assuming that they had not grasped the meaning. Any action which causes us to think more carefully about the teaching of Jesus is valuable.

The provision of an example

The line of approach moves from the greater to the lesser. If the Lord and Master has done this, the disciples cannot do less. The principle of doing what Jesus did has proved a valuable guide for Christian behaviour.

The underlining of a spiritual principle

It is socially accepted that the servant is not above the

master. There is real blessing in understanding aright the kind of master we have. We shall never emulate him until we see him as one who came among us to serve.

The warning against the betrayal
Jesus was preparing the disciples for the shock of discovering Judas' treachery. But even this is concluded with a further appeal for faith in Jesus himself. Again he associates his Father closely with him.

It was a difficult lesson to learn. No wonder the strange act needed to be explained. Have we yet grasped the spiritual principle involved?

JOHN 13:13
Our Lord and teacher

Wherever authority is exercised there must also be subjection. Where anyone rules others must obey. This is a principle in Christian life.

Jesus is an authoritative teacher
He speaks the truth of God. He speaks with perfect wisdom. Every believer acknowledges this fact. But it implies a willingness to obey that teaching.

Jesus is the believer's Lord
He has a sovereign claim on our obedience. We must confess him as Lord (Rom. 10:9).

Jesus expects his claims to be acknowledged
If we do, it must show in our actions. Jesus points us to his own example. You ought to do the same thing.

If we live as subjects of such a master it will

*improve our manner of life. Our aim will be
to please him rather than ourselves.*

JOHN 13:14
The importance of humility

*One of the Christian's worst enemies is pride.
To deal with it sometimes requires drastic
action. Jesus chose feet-washing to achieve it.*

Humility is not an option for the believer
This quality was not appreciated in the ancient world. It
was mistaken for weakness, as it often is today.

Humility means putting the needs of others first
Jesus thought of his disciples' comfort. This essentially
practical approach means our humility will be evident from
our actions rather than our words.

Humility does not pick and choose
No one would naturally go for feet-washing. Some would
regard it as beneath them. Christian leadership is often
guilty of a superiority attitude.

Humility has a supreme example
Jesus must have regarded humility as immensely important
since he chose such a method of demonstrating it. If he
stooped so low, why should we rate ourselves any higher?

*The meek inherit the earth, not the proud. No
wonder the wisdom of this world finds this
baffling.*

JOHN 13:15
I have given you an example

*Examples are invaluable in the learning
process. We cannot so easily grasp
instructions in the abstract. Jesus is expert at
the teaching technique.*

The character of the example
The disciples had lived with Jesus for some time. His whole
life had been an example in its perfection. But now they see
him performing a menial task.

The scope of the example
No one can fully emulate the example of Jesus. He had a
foreknowledge we do not possess. He was without sin. But
this act of humiliation is well within our scope.

*An example needs to be something or
someone who can be copied. This is why Jesus
sets out so practical a pattern. Even the
simplest can wash feet or do any other
similarly menial task.*

JOHN 13:21–30
Coping with treachery

*The spotlight falls not so much on Judas as on
Jesus. See how he handled the traitor among
the twelve. In this, as in the feet-washing, he
provides a pattern.*

An emotional reaction
Once again John notes that Jesus was troubled in spirit. He
was affected by those who turned against him. This human
reaction is comforting to those who have to pass through
similar experiences.

A startling revelation

John has already said that the devil had put it into the heart of Judas to betray him (verse 2). But now Jesus announces the betrayal.

An understandable perplexity

Peter beckons to John who asks Jesus, 'Who is it?' Matthew and Mark vividly bring out the perplexity. Each disciple in turn asks, 'Is it I?'

A significant gift

He was given the sop as an act of kindness. It may even be interpreted as an act of honour. Jesus utters no harsh words. John, writing years after the event, gives Judas' full name to avoid any possibility of confusion.

A tragic departure

Few words passed between Jesus and Judas, but enough to let Judas know that Jesus was aware of the treachery. Yet how discreet it all was in that the rest did not know. John tells us what some of them thought. The statement that Judas went out into the night is one of the saddest statements in Scripture.

Nothing is harder to bear than treachery among a circle of friends. This experience leaves many embittered. But Jesus points the way to a nobler approach.

JOHN 13:23
Reclining next to Jesus

The language is picturesque. One of the disciples leaned on Jesus' breast. This speaks of a close friendship with him.

He is called the disciple whom Jesus loved

Since John has said in verse 1 that Jesus loved all his own, this implies a special love for one of them, presumably John himself. If this identification is correct it would explain the sensitive portrayal of Jesus in this gospel.

He shows something of Jesus' human needs
His true humanity is seen in his human friendships. We have seen this in the case of the Bethany household and now among the inner circle of disciples.

He encourages us to seek closer relationship with Jesus
Jesus desires all disciples to be his friends (15:14, 15). John's experience can prove an inspiration even although the physical proximity has ceased.

The beloved disciple gained more than the rest because he sought to be near to Jesus.

JOHN 13:31–38
The time has come

Jesus was conscious of the march of time. The sense of approaching destiny is strongly brought out in this gospel.

The time of glorification
This is a familiar theme in John's gospel. The passion which loomed so near was not to be regarded as a tragedy but a triumph. Jesus' mind all along was on the resurrection. God's intention was to glorify his Son not to desert him.

The time of separation
Jesus knows his earthly life is drawing to a close. See how tenderly he drops the hint to his confused disciples!

The time for loving one another
In the dark hours ahead mutual loving support would be

crucial. But this new commandment has never been out-grown. The disciples of Jesus were to be known by their love.

The time for warning
Peter cannot cope with mysteries. 'Why can't I come with you, even if it does mean laying down my life?' Jesus knew the hollowness of these heroics. Peter was heading for a threefold denial. John 21 shows later how tenderly Jesus dealt with the lapse.

With all that Jesus had on his mind, he has concern for his disciples. John 14–16 demonstrates this. It is a universal truth. What he did and said then are still applicable to his people today.

JOHN 13:34, 35
The new commandment

Christians are no longer under law but under grace. Nevertheless Jesus talks of a commandment. Its basis however is different.

Its newness
The Decalogue urged love for God. Jesus summed up the law as love for God and for neighbour. But here he focuses on love among believers.

Its requirement
Loving one another is often stressed as a Christian duty. But all would admit its difficulty. We tend to love the lovable and avoid the unlovable. But this introduces quali-fications which Jesus did not allow.

Its pattern
The words 'even as I have loved you' make the task more difficult. This goes beyond normal human regard for

others. There must be the same kind of commitment to others which Jesus himself showed.

Its effect

It is so uncommon that everyone will notice. They will enquire for the source of such love. Where Christian love has faced up to the challenge, dramatic results have followed. 'See how these Christians love one another' was how some ancient pagans viewed their Christian contemporaries.

Perhaps we would be recognised as Christians more often and more effectively if our love for each other became deeper.

JOHN 14:1–7
Comfort for believers

The whole of the next section is intended to reassure the disciples. Jesus' impending death will involve them in a critical situation. He prepares them for it.

Jesus understands the problem

He knew their hearts would be troubled. He knows in advance what will afflict us.

Jesus reminds them of God's provision for them

They are exhorted simply to believe. Jesus' departure is to be for their good. The result will be a reuniting with him. This reunion is the most important aspect of the future. He had already told them the way he would take.

Jesus answers a real perplexity

Thomas expressed what they all must have thought. The fact is they had not grasped what he meant by the way. Another great 'I am' saying answers Thomas. Everything centres on Jesus. He is the only way to the Father.

The claims of Jesus here are far-reaching.
They are claims to uniqueness as the only way
to God. The way to see God was to see Jesus.
If these claims are not true they represent the
most appalling presumption.

JOHN 14:1–4
An antedote to distress of mind

Anxiety is a great robber of the peace that
believers ought to enjoy. These words of Jesus
have been a continuing source of
encouragement. Although they were
addressed to a particular situation they are
timeless in their application.

We are not expected to escape some kind of distress
We are in a fallen world and distress surrounds us. We
cannot hope to evade it, but we can rise above it.

We are assured that Jesus understands
The proverb says, 'A sorrow shared is a sorrow halved'. But
for believers in Jesus alleviation of the sorrow is possible.
Faith can banish unnecessary anxiety.

We are promised a secure future
Jesus has prepared a place for us. This throws some light on
our heavenly hope. But the greatest assurance is that where
he is we shall be. Included here is the further encouragement of the hope of Christ's return.

The disciples were faced with the physical
absence of Jesus. They discovered that he
would be closer to them after his death. That
discovery is made by every believer.

JOHN 14:4–6
I am the way

To want to know the way to God is a universal and continual quest. It also creates the most pressing questioning. How can we know the way?

Jesus himself is the way
He does not simply give directions like a route map. He goes ahead and leads the way. The only possibility of getting lost is in failing to follow.

Jesus is also the truth
A guide may be unreliable. His knowledge of the route may be defective. But Jesus not only knows truth but is truth. We can judge what is right by using him as the standard. This brings a personal dimension into ethics.

Jesus is the life
Even the best guide cannot lead those who are dead. But Jesus came to give life, to revitalise the spiritually dead. Through faith we find strength to follow.

Jesus leads us to the Father
God cannot be seen. His greatness cannot be grasped. But Jesus invites believers to look at him and see the Father through him.

God could not have provided an easier way for us to come to him. The message is 'Follow Jesus' and you will arrive.

JOHN 14:8–11
Philip's request

*The answer to Thomas' question leads to
further perplexity. Spiritual truths are difficult
to grasp and we may be grateful for the
queries raised by others.*

Show us the Father
Did Philip realise what he was asking for? What did he
expect? The opening of heaven? Or a transporting into
heaven? 'We shall be satisfied' seems incongruous in face of
such a stupendous request.

Philip had missed the point
Jesus wants Philip to think of the time he has spent with
him. Had he not seen the Father in him? Is there a tinge of
disappointment here in Jesus' words? Can the incarnate
Son live among men and yet they still seek the Father
elsewhere?

Jesus expounds his relationship with the Father
The close relationship (I in the Father, the Father in me)
should have been recognised. Jesus had often said his
words and works were the Father's. Do we identify with
the perplexity of the disciples? We are urged to believe, at
least because of what Jesus has done.

*Are we still asking for a view of the Father?
We shall find it in no other way than through
Jesus.*

JOHN 14:9
Knowing and yet not knowing

Acquaintance is often confused with true knowledge. We can know of a person without really knowing them. Jesus here applies this to himself.

Philip had accompanied Jesus through his ministry
Jesus had found him in Galilee (Jn. 1:43). Think of all he had witnessed since that initial calling. He must have become closely acquainted with what Jesus said and did.

Philip had failed to appreciate his true nature
He is representative of all the disciples. Does it baffle us how someone could be so near and yet so far? Yet such an experience has been many times repeated. We now know in a different way, and yet often our knowledge is superficial.

Philip was rebuked for his lack of understanding
How can you say, 'Show us the Father'? Jesus could have ignored the problem but he did not do so. He tenderly bears with our slowness to comprehend and provides further helps on the way.

What is the state of our knowledge? Can we really say we know Jesus in such a way that we see God in him?

JOHN 14:10–12
The works of Jesus

There is a fashion to treat what Jesus did as solely the works of a human being. But Jesus himself saw his works as powerful evidences of his divine origin.

The works are the works of the Father
The works were performed by the power of God through Jesus. They were evidence of a particular view of Jesus as the agent of divine power.

The works should lead to faith
The miracles used to be appealed to as an apologetic argument. This has been largely dropped. But John sees miracles as signs pointing to Jesus. They should lead to faith.

The works will be emulated by believers
The 'greater works' of the disciples would be to declare the mighty works of God to multitudes that they might believe in Jesus. God would be working through his people to achieve that result.

The works of Jesus are still taking place. Every time a person is converted it is his work through the Spirit.

JOHN 14:12–17
Great promises for the believer

*By his death and resurrection Jesus opens up
rich possibilities for those who believe in him.
These promises have been a continuing source
of comfort to believers ever since.*

The believer will do greater works
This seems incredible. Did Jesus mean greater miracles?
The book of Acts illustrates the point. The miracle of
conversions over a wide area exceeded the limited sphere
of Jesus' own operations. This followed the exaltation of
Jesus to the Father.

The believer will pray effective prayers
The key here is in the words 'in my name'. Any prayer in
the name and spirit of Jesus would be answered. Jesus'
promise concerns the extension of his work. Note the
repeated, 'I will do it'.

The believer will receive the Spirit of Truth
The gift of the Spirit is dependent on loving Jesus and
keeping his commandments. Love is demonstrated through
obedience. The Spirit of truth will be a Counsellor and will
dwell within believers.

*The disciples did not appreciate these
promises until after the resurrection. They are
still available for us. All God asks is faith,
love and obedience.*

JOHN 14:13
Prayer

Few become powerful in prayer. Most give insufficient attention to it. But we discover here what we miss.

The basic principle of prayer

The condition is asking in Jesus' name. What does this mean? If the name indicates the nature, the prayer must conform to Jesus' own pattern. How many of our prayers would this rule out?

The effectiveness of prayer

Prayer in Jesus' name is guaranteed to be answered. Does this seem impossible? Does it leave room for unanswered prayers? We must bear in mind that Jesus' way of doing what we ask may differ from our ideas. The promise is no guarantee that we can dictate to God.

The purpose of prayer

The Father must be glorified. Unless what we ask will do that, the promise does not hold. Sometimes our prayers go astray because we do not think enough about the Father's glory.

Most of us must find a challenge here. The prayers of the most devout sometimes fail to come up to this standard.

JOHN 14:16, 17
Another counsellor

*This gospel is rich in teaching about the Spirit.
This is the first of the Paraclete sayings. They
may be studied in isolation or in combination.*

The Spirit is given in response to the prayer of Jesus
There is here a remarkable statement about the relationship between the persons of the Godhead. Jesus
prays. The Father gives. The Spirit comes.

The Spirit will be a Counsellor
The word 'Paraclete' is difficult to define. It implies a
helper, an advocate, a comforter, a counsellor. The word
'another' is significant. Jesus had been all these. The Spirit
would continue what Jesus had already done.

The Spirit is the Spirit of Truth
The natural man finds it difficult to understand truth.
Pilate's question (18:38) is typical. The Spirit of truth is
an embarrassment to the world because of his absolute
standards. But the Christian has no option.

The Spirit will dwell within believers
Paul had much to say about this. No one could call Jesus
Lord except by the Spirit (1 Cor. 12:3). He dwells in every
believer. This means he is a constant guest and companion.

*Jesus' teaching on the Spirit is both reassuring
and challenging.*

JOHN 14:18–24
More assurances

*It is noticeable how often Jesus reiterates
similar spiritual truths. As an expert teacher
he knows the need for underlining difficult
concepts.*

You will see me
They will feel like orphans. But Jesus will not leave them.
They will 'see' him, as they did after the resurrection. The
sight came through awakened spiritual perception. We can
still receive that revelation.

You will know
Their knowledge of relationships was at present lacking. But after the resurrection all would be clarified. The
Christian knows that God was in Christ reconciling the
world (cf. 2 Cor. 5:18).

You will be loved by my Father
There are some simple conditions like keeping Jesus'
commandments. Yet all is enclosed in a spirit of love. The
Father's love, the Son's love, the believer's love are all in
view here. We keep his words because we love him.

Why us and not the world?
This was a fair question. Why this discrimination? Jesus'
answer is clear. The dividing line is the loving of Jesus and
the keeping of his word. The world excludes itself on this
test.

*There is an exclusiveness about Jesus which
we cannot escape. He sets himself as the sole
yardstick for the recipients of the promises of
God.*

JOHN 14:25–31
Jesus looks to the future

*In view of his impending departure, he looks
ahead to his disciples' needs.*

The Spirit will aid their memory
This was a practical necessity. The sayings of Jesus were
precious, and their memories would need jogging to recall
them. If this promise had not been given, we would not
have had the records in the gospels.

Jesus will give them his peace
He had no material possessions to bequeath to them. But
peace is infinitely more valuable. Many who lack nothing in
this world's wealth are desperately lacking in peace. The
Christian church still provides the strongest motivation
towards peace.

They will be expected to rejoice
His departure seemed to them to be a disaster. But love
sees further. Jesus was returning to the Father who was
greater than he. The disciples were warned and should not
have been surprised at his death.

The immediate experience of Jesus will not be failure
The ruler of this world might seem to have the upper hand
at the cross. But Jesus knows that the ruler has no power
over him. What he is doing is the Father's will.

*This was a crucial hour in world history.
Spiritual forces were pursuing the Messiah.
But the outcome was never in doubt.*

JOHN 14:25, 26
The spirit as teacher

Here is a different view of the Spirit. It is most valuable in view of our dullness of understanding. Truth needs a competent teacher.

The Spirit's qualification to teach
To teach all things, the Spirit must know all things. The teacher must know more than the disciple. The Spirit knows the whole of truth, because he is the Spirit of Truth.

The Spirit's mission to teach
He would be sent by the Father for this purpose. We do not appoint our own teacher. But we know we have been given the best of all possible teachers. Our task is to be teachable.

The Spirit's aid in the processes of recall
Jesus addresses those who had heard him. How much had they remembered? The Spirit would sharpen the mental processes. The 'all' at the end of the verse is suggestive. Were there no teachings they forgot? It probably means all the vital information.

The apostles could not do without the Spirit's aid. Neither can we in spite of the records we possess that they never had. The Spirit still recalls the teaching of Jesus.

JOHN 15:1–8
The vine

*This is a kind of extended parable like that of
the good shepherd. It has an application in
several parts.*

Christ as the vine
The figure is a natural one for Palestine. Compare the Old
Testament example of Israel (Isa. 5). It was used as a
symbol of the nation. The true vine is the new stem from
which the church comes. Christ is the source of its spiritual
life.

The disciples as branches
The vine depends on its branches. They depend on it for sap
and life. But there must be close contact. Jesus calls it
abiding or remaining in him.

The process of pruning
Fruitfulness follows from correct pruning. It is hard but
necessary. It is a vivid illustration. But in what ways does
the Father prune? All the experiences of life are intended
to contribute to our greater fruitfulness. The branch not
abiding in Christ is no true branch and is cast out and burnt.

The necessity for fruitfulness
Why bother? A fruitless tree only cumbers the ground. It
may be an attractive vine, but it is the fruit which matters.
The fruit brings glory to God. What is the fruit? Perhaps the
fruit of the Spirit (Gal. 5:22).

*When the vinedresser comes will he be
disappointed in our fruitfulness? Will the
Father be glorified?*

JOHN 15:1, 2
The vinedresser

*The idea of God as keeping a vineyard
teaches some deep truths about him.*

God's care for his vineyard

His works are always good. He never bungles his programme. He loves his people and is concerned for their
welfare.

God's treatment of the branches

He examines the branches. He cut out the useless wood. He
looks for close connection with the stem. His pruning is
always wise. He is the expert horticulturist.

God's expectation from his people

The plan is for fruit. A vineyard needs to be productive.
The lives of his followers are intended to show fruit. He
looks for a good crop. Is he disappointed?

*He always desires the best for us. When we
feel the pruning knife it hurts, but God has a
purpose in it.*

JOHN 15:5
Apart from Christ

*The non-Christian world by definition lives
'apart from Christ'. Life apart from him has
fewer moral challenges or restraints. But Jesus
is here addressing his own followers.*

No approach to God

Jesus has demonstrated this in John 14. He is the only way
to God. All other methods are futile.

No worthwhile purpose

What can be achieved is described as nothing. All human efforts lead nowhere, for there is no lasting satisfaction.

No effective fruitfulness

Whatever is achieved is not the fruit of the Spirit. Some moral values may appear, but the desire to glorify God is absent. Life becomes mainly self-pleasing.

The negative aspects are valuable in drawing attention to the wonderful experience of living in Christ.

JOHN 15:9–11
Remaining in love

Jesus has much to say about love in this gospel. It is a key word in relationships as is seen here.

The Father loves the Son

This sets the pattern for the kind of love Jesus is talking about. This is love at the highest level. It is a love which freely gives.

The Son loves his disciples

The same quality of love is focused on the followers of Jesus. His love is no less than the Father's love.

The disciples must remain in this love

Love of such quality is so attractive that it should require little effort to remain basking in it. Why do we so easily forget?

The Son remains in the Father's love

Jesus knows our need for illustration. If we want to know what remaining in love means, look at his relation with the Father. This is life of the purest kind.

163

These loving relationships result in great joy
To remain in the love of Christ is the surest way to fullness of joy. Love and joy are inseparably linked.

Here is a theme which is inexhaustible. It presents a target which we never attain but which acts as a continual spur.

JOHN 15:11
Joy

Jesus speaks here of 'my joy' and 'your joy'. The two are joined together in the experience of the believer.

Consider the joy of Jesus
Bearing in mind his knowledge of the approaching passion, why should he have joy? Perhaps Heb. 12:2 provides the answer. His mission was the joyous one of drawing many to God. His joy was the joy of bringing immeasurable blessing to others.

Experience the joy of Jesus
Jesus' teaching is directed to this end. There is a direct line of communication between his joy and ours. That joy is infectious. Those closest to him cannot escape the exhilaration of his wonderful joy.

Develop that joy to the full
Whatever Jesus gives he gives unstintingly. This is not some passing experience, but a growing one. Once we taste the joy we relish more of it. A fully joyful Christian is one who will radiate the joy to others.

Our sorrowful world cannot see too much of this Christian joy. But how much does it see? Is the world a brighter place because of us?

JOHN 15:12–17
You are my friends

Friendship always involves two people. It suggests a mutual relationship. When Jesus uses it of his disciples it presents a challenge.

Christian friendship is based on love

The command to love was given in 13:34. It is repeated here, so important does Jesus consider it to be. Loving one another is difficult, but is essential to true Christian friendship. We cannot choose the objects of love.

Real love is prepared to be sacrificial. That is the kind of love Jesus has for us. He died for his friends.

Christian friendship arises from friendship with Christ

We graduate from servants to friends. This means that Christ shares his plans and his thoughts with us. Once we learn to relate to him, the inter-relation with others will be a reflection of this. How far do we enter into what Jesus shares with his friends?

Friendship with Christ is not our choice but his

In any friendship someone has to take the initiative. It has to begin somewhere. That initiative is with Christ. How would we ever have become his friends unless he had taken the first step?

Friendship with Christ has some conditions

It is a matter of fruitfulness. The vine imagery is still in mind. If the fruit is the fruit of the Spirit, it means the process of becoming more like Christ. It is the picture of two friends becoming more alike. They even share the same access to the Father.

How do we respond to his invitation to become his friends? Are we prepared for the consequences?

JOHN 15:15
Servants and friends

*When we become friends of Jesus we do not
cease to be servants. We need to think about
the relation between the two roles.*

The role of servant
Jesus' feet washing act was intended to teach the disciples
to serve. Is there a difference here? Jesus may not call us
servants but we are called to serve. Jesus was the Servant
par excellence. We cannot be greater than he is. Paul called
himself the slave of Jesus Christ. Christians regard any
work for God as service.

The role of friend
Jesus states the difference between the servant and the
friend. The servant is not asked in at the planning stage,
whereas the friend is. The servant acts on orders, but the
friend shares the burdens of the master.

The relation between them
The suggestion seems to be that the disciple performs both
functions. He discovers the mind of the master and he
happily puts it into practice. The Master does not treat us as
slaves. He desires fellowship with us.

*The idea of servant-friend is shunned by most
masters because of the fear of a lessening of
respect. But Jesus takes the risk.*

JOHN 15:16
Choice and appointment

*Many are worried about the thought of the
divine choice. They are scared of losing their
freedom. But Jesus himself claims the
freedom to choose. This verse may help us to
understand why.*

You did not choose me
The disciples would know this. Jesus' mission was such an
enigma to them that if the choice had been left to them
probably none would have followed.

But I chose you
Jesus is clearly not putting himself on a level with his
disciples. He was the master planner. The mission of Jesus
was not the result of a committee decision. His choice of
companions is mystifying, particularly the choice of Judas.
But even there Jesus himself is in control.

And appointed you
The future mission of the church depended on these men. It
was they who were to go and bear fruit. Humanly speaking
it was not promising. But these same men did spread the
good news far and wide. We should never cease to marvel
at the appointments of God.

*Do you imagine that God would never choose
you for his work? Think again, for his choices
are often baffling to human wisdom.*

JOHN 15:18–21
Exposure to the world

*Here in summary form is a record of the
antagonism between the church and the world
throughout the centuries.*

Hated by the world
The 'world' here is the human world apart from God. It is
linked with hate towards the mission of Jesus and towards
his disciples. Hate implies more than apathy. It is a word of
antagonism. We are in an alien environment.

Chosen out of the world
Although still in the same environment, the disciples are
separate from it. Their new method of life and thought will
draw the opposition of the world against them. History
bears abundant testimony to the reality of this fact.

Persecuted by the world
Society cannot tolerate those who challenge its spiritual
standards. Even otherwise benevolent communities have
waxed hostile against the followers of Jesus. The persecution may take various forms but its motive is the same –
intense dislike of the uncomfortable teaching of Jesus.

*The world will never welcome the Christian
with open arms. If it is tolerant it may be that
the Christian witness is not sufficiently clear.
There is always implicit alienation even if it
has not surfaced.*

JOHN 15:22–27
Without excuse

*There is strong language and strong challenge
here. Rejection of the witness of Jesus is
condemned in the strongest manner.*

The difference that the coming of Jesus has made

(a) 'If I had not come.' Since the coming of Jesus they
have no excuse if they continue in sin. This implies
that before there was some excuse for them. But as a
result of the incarnation unbelief in Jesus is regarded
as sin.

(b) 'If I had not done the works.' To have seen the
unique works of Jesus puts the onus on the observer.
He must form an opinion. He is now answerable if he
rejects the challenge. No one else did such works as
Jesus did. It was an inestimable privilege to have
seen them.

His witness has resulted in hate

Those who reject Jesus are regarded as haters of him and of
the Father. Many who ignore the claims of Jesus would be
surprised that their indifference is interpreted as hate. But
this confirms that a neutral position is impossible. Hate in
New Testament language is the absence of love. To hate
without cause is not new. The Old Testament speaks of it.

His witness is about to be reinforced

(a) *By the witness of the Spirit*. Do we think that those
who were in personal contact with Jesus had the
greater condemnation? Jesus reminds us that the
witness is still present, for the Spirit who comes from
the Father will also witness to himself. We are still
without excuse.

(b) *By the witness of the disciples*. Jesus tells them they
are witnesses. They had lived with Jesus. They had
much to tell. Some of them wrote things down for
our benefit.

*It is a serious matter to reject the most
wonderful testimony in the world to the most
wonderful person. Those who lightly treat this
stupendous revelation have no possible
excuse.*

JOHN 15:26, 27
The witness of the spirit

*This is the third of Jesus' Paraclete sayings in
this gospel. Each adds its own insight and this
points to witnessing.*

The promised Spirit

(a) Jesus sends the Spirit from the Father. This points to
harmony among the persons of the trinity.

(b) The Spirit is the Spirit of truth. Truth is of utmost
importance in witnessing.

(c) The Spirit proceeds from the Father. The words are
difficult, but they establish the exalted origin of the
Spirit.

(d) The Spirit bears witness to Christ. Nowhere in the
New Testament does the Spirit draw attention to
himself. He is always pointing to Christ.

The communicating disciples

The disciples' witness is distinct from the witness of the
Spirit. But it is closely linked. Our witness is imperfect; the
Spirit's is perfect. We forget too easily; the Spirit never
forgets. We tend to draw attention to ourselves; the Spirit
always points to Christ.

*If the future of the church had depended on
the faltering witness of the disciples the
outlook would have been bleak. But the
combination of human testimony and the
Spirit's witness is unstoppable.*

JOHN 16:1–4
Predictions of persecutions

The disciples were facing a critical period.
Jesus warns of approaching persecution. It
was only later that the reality dawned on
their minds.

Warning against a coming stumbling block

Jesus aimed to prepare the disciples for a shock. If we see a stumbling block ahead there is more possibility of avoiding it. But warnings of confrontations are never readily received.

The nature of the coming persecution

The disciples will face excommunication. This would amount to religious censure. The religious authorities would act in this way for fear that their status quo would be threatened. Religious opposition to the cause of Christ has often been most intense, and indeed still is.

The motive for the persecution

Many savage attacks on the followers of Christ have been carried out in the belief that God was being served. Saul of Tarsus is the classical example. How easy it is to think that we serve God and yet in effect to oppose him! The reason is lack of understanding of the Father's will.

The value of the warning

Jesus knew how valuable memory of his warnings and promises would be. The more we dwell on his words the greater the possibility of recalling them in times of opposition.

The 'hour' has come to many groups and in
many periods of history. Today many are
suffering for their faith in Christ strengthened
by his word.

JOHN 16:5–11
Advantages from Christ's departure

The death and resurrection of Jesus marks the beginning of a new epoch. The disciples were in the transition stage.

His departure was a traumatic event for them
They wanted to continue as now. The thought of losing Jesus was distressing. It was best not to pursue it. They refrained from asking 'Where are you going?' Yet Jesus knew the sorrow in their hearts.

Yet his departure would result in the gift of the Spirit
The Counsellor would come only subsequent to the death of Christ. This points to Pentecost when their sorrow would be turned to joy.

The Spirit would bring conviction to the world
This promise was intended to encourage them. They would not be able to convince people after Jesus' departure, but the Spirit would. The book of Acts illustrates the point.

Although he has gone to the Father, he did not intend his followers to be forsaken. The coming of the Spirit would more than make up for the lack of his physical presence.

JOHN 16:5–7
Sorrow

*There are many different reactions to the
teaching of Jesus. The idea of his leaving them
filled the disciples with dismay. They never
grasped that it was part of God's plan.*

They failed to understand the mission of Jesus
There is a touch of reproof in Jesus' words. They lacked the
enquiring spirit. They showed no concern for the needs of
Jesus. They were not facing up to reality.

Yet sorrow filled their hearts because of what they heard
It was understandable. They evidently thought it was
rational to be sorrowful. They had become overburdened
with their own disadvantages.

Nevertheless it was for their advantage that Jesus died
The priceless gift of the Spirit was the direct sequel to the
death of Jesus (cf. 7:39). The disciples were to learn later
how the Spirit would dispel their sorrow.

*Although we cannot avoid sorrow, we can
conquer it. We should contemplate what Jesus
has done for us.*

JOHN 16:8–11
The Spirit's work of conviction

*Elsewhere the Spirit's work is in believers.
Here alone there is reference to his work in
unbelievers. Unless the Spirit convicts there
will be no awakening of conscience.*

Conviction of sin

There is a notorious reluctance to admit sin. People will
think up all manner of excuses to explain it away. It has
even become unpopular in theology because of the inroads
of psychology.

The Christian view of sin is that all are guilty of it. Here
sin is pin-pointed as unbelief in Christ. It is the Spirit's work
to convince people of this.

Conviction of righteousness

This must be the righteousness which is the result of what
Jesus did on the cross and what took place at the resurrec-
tion. This is implied in the reference to his going to the
Father.

Most people's idea of righteousness is what can be
achieved by their own efforts. To accept a total dependence
on the righteousness of Christ requires the Spirit's work.

Conviction of judgment

The judgment in view is the overthrow of the ruler of this
world. This heralds the ultimate `triumph of good. In a
world still dominated by evil it needs the Spirit to convince
us that the forces of evil are already defeated.

*Unbelievers will never come to faith as a result
of human persuasion without the powerful
convicting agency of the holy Spirit. Sin,
righteousness and judgment must be dealt with
in any presentation of the gospel.*

JOHN 16:12–15
The Spirit as guide

*This is the last Paraclete saying in John. It is a
preparation for the work and witness of the
disciples. Guidance is a difficult subject for the
Christian. Here are some signposts.*

The need for the guide
Jesus is concerned to steer his people into truth. He knew
how easily error creeps in, for he warns against it. But
unaided we cannot distinguish spiritual truth from error.

The promise of the guide
The Spirit of truth is well qualified to lead into truth. He is a
guide who knows the way. There is no possibility for the
Spirit straying from the truth since it is his nature.

The authority of the guide
Every teacher must have his authorities. Our guide tells us
what he has himself received. In this operation the three
persons of the Trinity are involved. The Spirit speaks with
the authority of Christ.

The objective of the guide
The Spirit will glorify Jesus. His activities are devoted to
this end. Whatever passes for his work which does not
glorify Jesus is not a true work of the Spirit. This provides
us with a yardstick with which to test.

*The Spirit glorifies the Son. The Son glorifies
the Father. The Father glorifies the Son
(17:5). But no one is said to glorify the Spirit.*

JOHN 16:16–24
Sorrow turned to joy

This promise of transformation is a great encouragement. Sorrow is universal and any means that can replace it with joy must be of infinite value.

The perplexity

The statement of Jesus in verse 16 must have seemed confusing. The disciples have to confess 'We don't know what he means'. The encouragement here is that Jesus knew their perplexity. Christians with perplexities may take courage from this.

The sorrow

The tables will be turned. The world may rejoice at first but the disciples will weep. This will be the reaction to the events of the cross. Why is the way so painful? Jesus uses the illustration of child birth.

The joy

What will cause such a change from pain to rejoicing? The mother rejoices at the sight of her child. The disciples will rejoice at the sight of Jesus. That joy is so secure that no one can take it away. Moreover the joy can be increased through prayer in Jesus' name. Experience of answered prayer brings fullness of joy.

Jesus himself discovered the change of his own sorrow into joy (Heb. 12:2). Our sorrow is nothing like his, but he shares his joy with us.

JOHN 16:22
I will see you again

See how Jesus comforted his disciples just before his death. His words have a message of encouragement for us.

The occasion

After the cross some saw him on the Easter morning. They all saw him during the following days. His rising from the dead made all the difference. What had seemed a disaster was turned into a triumph.

The result

Your hearts will rejoice. No one could have foreseen such a result from so cruel an event. But the overcoming of the ruler of this world was something to be celebrated. Ever since then Christians in all ages have rejoiced to celebrate the resurrection day.

There is no greater theme for rejoicing than the triumph of the resurrection.

JOHN 16:23, 24
Successful prayer

Most people find it hard to pray. It is harder still to be convinced that God will answer. Here is an assurance which will help us.

A sense of need

The kind of prayer in mind here is not prayer from a sense of duty. It was the kind that sprang from sorrow. Basic to all true prayer is a recognition of our own weakness.

A readiness to ask

'Ask anything of the Father' seems remarkably comprehensive. But the condition is important. It must be in Jesus' name, which implies according to his wishes. The 'anything' becomes immeasurably ennobled.

An assurance of result

'Ask and you will receive' is a promise which leads to complete confidence. But what about unanswered prayer? It may be our unanswered prayers are prayers not asked according to the condition. This assurance does not apply to those.

The magnitude of our prayers will reflect our view of the magnitude of the one to whom we come.

JOHN 16:25–33
Plain speaking

Jesus adapted his words to the needs of his audiences. Illustrations were used where understanding was limited. But the time for plain speaking must come.

Plain teaching about the Father

(a) He loves the disciples. Jesus had said this before. But here it underlines the Father's willing response to the prayers of his people. Note the reason for the Father's love – because of their love for Jesus. We are reminded that God delights in those who honour the Son.

(b) He sent the Son into the world. 'I came from the Father' shows Jesus' clear consciousness of his origin. 'I am going to the Father' speaks of his confidence in the future. The cross which stands between is not mentioned.

Plain warnings about the future

The disciples affirm their belief that Jesus had come from God, but he issues a solemn warning. He would be left alone. His disciples would all run away. That would be hurtful to Jesus, but the Father would be with him. But the disciples would later experience another kind of scattering (Acts 8:1).

The concluding words of verse 33 have been a constant encouragement to the followers of Jesus. There is no doubt about the issue.

JOHN 16:26, 27
The Father's love

The use of a human analogy here is valuable. Most people have known something of a human father's love. Those who have not will find more difficulty in appreciating the teaching here.

The Father loves you

This statement is at the heart of the gospel. That is why he sent his Son. The whole process of salvation springs from God's love.

Because you have loved me

Does this mean that God's love for us depends on our prior love for Christ? It cannot. These words make clear that those whom he specially loves are those in a relationship with Christ. They are believers.

We cannot dwell too much on the Father's love. This is the greatest revelation which Jesus came to give. God is not one to be feared but one to love and be loved.

JOHN 16:28
The history of Jesus in a nutshell

Here is Jesus' own view of his life's mission. It is masterly for its brevity.

He came from the Father
Notice how often in John's gospel this fact is emphasised. Any attempt to understand his life from any other starting point will lead to distortion. Jesus begins with his pre-existence.

He came into the world
This sums up the incarnation. The Word became flesh and dwelt among us. This points to his humanity. It also points to the object of his mission.

He left the world
The leaving would involve a cross. It would happen in a violent way. But here it is the fact which is important. The mission required him to leave as much as to come.

He returned to the Father
This sums up the resurrection and the ascension, which are linked to provide a triumphal home-coming. The cycle of redemption was then completed.

It is striking how different Jesus' view of his own life is from that of many observers. We shall never properly appreciate what he did until we see it in his own framework.

JOHN 16:32
The loneliness of Jesus

*There is pathos in the words 'you will leave me
alone'. They remind us that Jesus walked a
solitary path in accomplishing his mission.
Yet there is another side to that loneliness.*

His loneliness in the world
He lived among us, yet he was different from us. His moral
superiority meant an inevitable clash with his environment.
Even his closest friends could not grasp his mission. They
scattered and left him to face the cross alone.

His companionship with the Father
His loneliness would have been intolerable had it not been
that the Father was with him. When men forsook him the
Father never did. The cry on the cross was real anguish
because of the close relationship between Father and Son.

*If Jesus discovered a means of overcoming
loneliness, the same method must work for all
who experience loneliness. No circumstances
can impede the Father's companionship with
his own people.*

JOHN 16:33
Overcoming the world

*The Christian knows that he is in an alien
environment. This is the sense of the word
'world' in this context.*

The followers of Christ are in the world
Jesus never suggested that they would escape the adverse
effects of their environment. The church continues to
witness in the world.

The followers of Christ will meet tribulation
Because of the nature of the Christian message opposition
to it is unavoidable. The world of men always resorts
to intimidating tactics when faced with unpalatable
challenges.

The followers of Christ will receive encouragement
We face a defeated foe. The world is not the master. Jesus
claims to have overcome it. When opposition is intense this
assurance is of great value. We are on the winning side.

*Compared with the weakness of the Church
the world seems overwhelmingly powerful. It
takes faith in Christ to be convinced it is
already defeated.*

JOHN 17:1–5
Christ's special prayer for himself

*The whole of this chapter contains what is
perhaps the most profound prayer in the New
Testament. It was uttered at a time of crisis.
This section of it, the smallest part, is a prayer
of Jesus for himself.*

The intimate nature of the prayer
Note the uplifted eyes and the simple address of 'Father'.
There was no barrier between them. There was direct
access.

The purpose of the prayer
It is a case of mutual glorification. There is no greater glory
than that which belongs to God. But the request of Jesus for
a restoration of the original glory helps us to understand
what was in the mind of Jesus as he faced the cross.

The basis of the prayer
Jesus recalls certain facts. He has been given power. His power is to give eternal life. This consists of knowing God and his Son. This amounts to a summary of the mission of Jesus. He claims the job is done. This is a powerful plea.

How near do our prayers approach the example of Jesus in being concerned about the glory of God?

JOHN 17:1–5
Jesus' idea of glory

Ambition drives people to seek their own glory. What glory they achieve is ephemeral. The only one who sought his own glory and achieved it permanently was Jesus.

Glory was concerned with achieving something for others
The prayer for glory was answered on a cross. This is a reversal of normal assessments. Glory is inseparable from the most total act of self-giving.

Glory was seen in the earthly life of Jesus
John has already mentioned this. Cf. 1:14 'we have seen his glory'. And note also the glory seen in the miracles (cf. 2:11; 11:4). The human life of Jesus was a glorious life.

No other person has ever shone with such glory as Jesus. It is a glory which has not been dimmed by the passing of time.

JOHN 17:2,3
The authority of Jesus

*There is a mystery in this passage. It is the
problem why all do not receive eternal life.
But all that Jesus implies is that God who
gives alone knows the answer.*

He possessed power over all
The authority he has comes from God. This means his
power is real power. When he spoke or acted it was with
authority. His authority was most evident in spiritual
matters.

He gives eternal life to some
The gift is limited by the Father's choice. It was given to all
whom the Father had given to him. But the gift has not been
received by all flesh. The mystery is baffling. But it is a fact
of life that many reject the gift.

He defines eternal life as knowledge
It is not equated to general knowledge, but to knowledge of
God and of Christ. He did not impart such knowledge to all
but only to those ready to receive it. There is an inseparable
link between faith and knowledge.

*We should not permit the mystery of God's
choice to prevent us from receiving the gift.
The very desire to possess it is evidence of
God's work in our hearts.*

JOHN 17:6–19
Christ's prayer for his disciples

Here is a marvellous prayer of Jesus for his disciples. It reveals a great deal about his concern for them. It serves as a reminder of his continual intercession for us.

The basis of the prayer
Jesus appeals to what he has already done for them.
- (a) He has revealed the Father's name to them (verse 6).
- (b) He has given them the Father's words (verses 8, 14).
- (c) He has kept them in the Father's name (verse 12).
- (d) He is going to the Father (verses 11, 13).
- (e) He has consecrated himself for them (verse 19).

The status of the disciples
Jesus notes how important the disciples are.
- (a) They belong to God (verses 6, 9).
- (b) They know the relationship between Father and Son (verses 7, 8).
- (c) They glorify Christ (verse 10).

The content of the prayer
Jesus makes three specific requests.
- (a) Keep them in my name that they may be one (verse 11).
- (b) Keep them from the evil one (verse 15).
- (c) Sanctify them in the truth (verse 17).

This prayer can never be wholly comprehended. It furnishes ample food for thought. Is this the kind of prayer we are used to praying on behalf of the church?

JOHN 17:6–10
The high priest pleads for his people

This petition contains a great deal of information. Jesus was not informing God. He rather sets out clearly the grounds for his prayer.

The status of his people
   (a) They are separated from the world.
   (b) They are the property of the Father.
   (c) They are the Father's gift to the Son.

The evidence of his people
   (a) They know that Christ's works are God's works.
   (b) They know the value of his words.
   (c) They know that God has sent him.

The security of his people
   (a) They are secure through Christ's prayers for them.
   (b) They are doubly protected since they belong to both Father and Son.

This prayer is a pattern of our high priest's constant prayers for his people.

JOHN 17:15
A negative and positive prayer

It is valuable to note the form in which Jesus expresses this prayer. Perhaps we are not too familiar with negative forms of prayer.

The negative
'I do not pray.' Why should such a statement be included in

this prayer? It is to strengthen the positive statement that follows. Removal from the world is not what any of the disciples would have desired. But Jesus has a specific reason for wanting them in the world.

They were to be his witnesses. His work was to continue through them. However antagonistic the world was, it was necessary for the disciples to witness to it.

The positive
'Keep them from the evil one.' There is bound to be continual tension between the followers of Christ and their environment. But the prayer that God would keep them from the attacks of evil forces is a great encouragement. In the spiritual battle it is God, not his people, against the evil one.

This prayer reminds us that the Christian life demands courage. There is no escape route but ample resources for the continuation of the struggle.

The negative disposes of what might seem the easy way. But the positive faces the issue and leads to victory.

JOHN 17:20–26
Christ's prayer for others

If the last section of the prayer has concentrated on the immediate disciples of Jesus, this section looks ahead to those who were later to believe.

He prays for all his people
The scope of the prayer is universal. The long line of witnesses beginning with the apostles still continues. The modern church is included in this prayer.

He prays for the unity of his people
The pattern of unity is no less than the unity of Father and

Son. Unity is to be distinguished from uniformity. The foundation of unity is to be 'in us' which involves an identification with the mind of Father and Son.

He prays that the world may know through his people
The prayer for unity has a purpose – that the world may believe and know what God is doing. Unity based on a right understanding of God's purpose in Christ is a powerful influence in the world.

He prays that his people may be with him
Jesus wants them to see his glory. That glory goes back before creation. He looks towards it through the cross.

We have here a glimpse of the sort of prayer our heavenly high priest makes for us.

JOHN 17:20–23
A prayer for unity

With the divided state of the church today, much interest centres in the quest for unity. All would admit the desirability of this, but on what terms? Jesus' prayer helps to put it into a right perspective.

Its scope
All believers are involved. The 'all' in verse 21 is comprehensive. The family of God was intended to be a united family. It includes everyone who truly believes in Christ of whatever nation or ethnic origin.

Its model
The unity of Father and Son is the yardstick. This puts the type of unity involved on the highest possible level. It is above mere uniformity or structural unity. It means a unity of minds.

Its means

Note the phrase 'believe in me'. There is no question of unity apart from a living relationship to Christ. The believer becomes united with Christ and therefore united with other believers.

Its purpose

The aim is to perfect the unity of believers. Jesus sees this as an important factor in the impact of the gospel on the world to lead it to believe that God has sent Jesus and to know that God has loved him. Unless church unity achieves this aim, it is not true unity.

Church unity is a laudable quest, but we must be sure our ideas of unity are the same as those of Jesus.

JOHN 17:22–24
Sharing the glory

Man's idea of glory is usually to be acclaimed by his fellows. But there is a nobler concept in this prayer of Jesus.

Jesus has already given glory to the disciples

What has already been given by Jesus is not the special position of the apostles. It is the glory of becoming a member of the Christian community. Every believer shares the same glory.

Jesus prays that they may see his glory

Earlier in the prayer Jesus has mentioned the glory he had from the beginning. His earthly existence had temporally obscured it. But a time would come when the disciples' eyes would be opened.

Jesus wants his disciples to share his greater glory

His desire is to have his people with him. There can be no

greater glory for them than this. The Christian hope for a heavenly inheritance is based not simply on our desire, but on Christ's own wish.

Glory is not something reserved for the future. We can experience it now. A taste of it will whet the appetite for future glory.

JOHN 17:25, 26
O righteous Father

The righteousness of God is an important part of the Christian teaching about God. When Jesus calls his Father righteous he is affirming this truth.

Jesus appealed to the character of God
In this he sets an example for us. The effectiveness of any prayer will depend on the conception of God on which it is based.

He distinguishes the world from the disciples
The world is ignorant of God's nature, but the disciples are not. They know that God has sent Jesus. The distinction must be recognised in our communication with the world. The gospel is faced with a world which is spiritually ignorant.

He wants the Father's love to be in them
It is wrong to suppose that concern for righteousness will exclude love. Love must come from a worthy source. The love of the righteous Father is a love of the highest possible value.

Do not shy away from the thought of a just God, for an unjust God would be terrifying. Make this a basic element in prayer.

JOHN 18:1–11
The arrest of Jesus

John does not record the agony of Jesus in Gethsemane as the other evangelists do. But there is still poignancy in the account of the arrest.

The scene

The garden of Gethsemane was on the slopes of the mount of Olives. Jesus and his disciples knew it well. Jesus was aware what would happen if he went there, but he persisted with his mission. He would not be deflected from his appointed task.

The soldiers

As Judas leads the attack, consisting of soldiers and some of the religious officers, the peace of the garden was disturbed. They clearly feared Jesus might escape. They brought their weapons as if to arrest a dangerous man.

The seeking

Jesus took the initiative. He twice asked the approaching officers, 'Whom do you seek?' Their falling back was dramatic as if the appearance and the majestic words of Jesus overawed them. They were probably astonished that he made no effort to avoid them.

The sword

Peter's impulsive swipe at the slave's ear leads to a rebuke from Jesus. What did Peter think he would achieve? He was acting outside the plan of God. Even a slave's ear was important to Jesus.

The arrest was man's way of dealing with the saviour of the world. But Jesus rejects the need for violent means. He shows himself to be the prince of peace.

JOHN 18:1, 2
A garden of destiny

A garden on the slopes of the mount of Olives
was the scene of happenings which deeply
affected subsequent history. It holds a place of
special importance for us still.

Consider the importance of the garden for Jesus
During the public ministry he took his disciples aside privately. He had just spent time with them in the upper room. And during the passion week in Jerusalem he had often used the garden of Gethsemane, where he could be alone with them amid the calm of nature. For him the garden was a place of peace.

Consider the significance of the garden for the disciples
At least three of them heard the strong cries and saw the drops of blood. John does not mention this, but he could not have forgotten it. Ever afterwards Gethsemane would be associated with the sorrow of Jesus.

Consider the place of the garden in the mind of Judas
It was the place for his act of treachery. He could hardly have chosen a more sacred place. But for him the mission of Jesus was of no importance. The same garden that witnessed the tears of Jesus saw the kiss of Judas.

Consider the place in the plans of Jesus' opponents
It was where Jesus was arrested. For them it was a place of triumph. They thought they had defeated him. But they were reckoning apart from God.

Gethsemane is still a symbol for the conflicts
in human minds. It is the garden of human
destiny where Jesus embraces the full
consequences of his saving work.

JOHN 18:8, 9
The unselfishness of Jesus

*It was the hour of crisis for Jesus. He had
already passed through inner turmoil over the
coming passion. Yet his thoughts are
nevertheless on others.*

He disregarded his own safety
He knew precisely what was happening. The events of the
cross did not come as a disillusionment. He knew it was all
part of a plan. His attitude before his captors is regal in its
acceptance of danger.

He sought the safety of his followers
It was essential for the success of the ongoing mission that
the disciples should be spared. At this critical point he
showed great concern over them.

His action was seen as a fulfilment of his prediction
In his prayer he had stated that none would be lost (17:12).
He was taking action to ensure that this was fulfilled. His
action here is surely exemplary for all in showing the way of
self-sacrifice.

*Because Jesus faced the threat and submitted
to it, mankind gained a redeemer. In carrying
out that task he provides a pattern to follow.
He thought more of others than of himself.*

JOHN 18:10, 11
The vanity of violence

*In days when the nations of the world pile up
deadly armaments and men of violence
terrorise societies, this passage has much to
say about Jesus' approach.*

The methods of attack
The mob came with weapons and torches. It was their only
resort. There was no room for persuasion or reasoning.
They thought only in terms of violence. Theirs was the
philosophy that might is right, a philosophy that still holds
sway in our modern world.

The methods of defence: the way of Peter
Peter produces a sword. He shows at once he shares the
same philosophy of violence as the attackers. His years with
Jesus had taught him nothing of a better way. Did he obtain
the sword as a result of what Jesus had said (Lk. 22:38)? If
so he had badly misunderstood. This was not Jesus' way.

The methods of defence: the way of Jesus
He gives himself up without a fight. To the natural mind this
was sheer defeatism. But Jesus knew better. His cause lives
on while his attackers are pitied for their lack of understanding. The yielding of Jesus was not to a crowd of armed
soldiers, but to a task that would save the world.

*It may be questioned whether violence ever
achieves anything. Jesus pointed out that those
who take the sword will perish by it. History
bears this out. Any discussion of the modern
nuclear scene should take full account of this.*

JOHN 18:11
The sword and the cup

These two things may be regarded as symbolic. They are mutually exclusive and a choice must be made between them.

The sword rejected

This was symbolic of physical force. Many causes have been furthered by being forcibly thrust on unwilling recipients. But the results have been oppressive. The Christian church was not to be launched that way. 'Put your sword into its sheath' is still the principle for the furtherance of the gospel.

The cup accepted

This was symbolic of an allotted task. To accept one's cup was to accept one's destiny. Moreover the cup was given by the Father. The cup was the way of the cross, the way of self-giving, not the way of physical attack. The cup has baffled the opponents of Christianity ever since.

The instrument of the gospel has never been violence. It advances by the method of persuasion and self-sacrifice.

JOHN 18:12–14; 19–24
Before the high priests

When Jesus stands before the high priests, it is they rather than he who are judged.

The partiality of Caiaphas

John notes that Caiaphas had advised the death of Jesus as an act of expediency (Jn. 11:49ff). This was the man who was to try him. He had already made up his mind.

The curiosity of Annas

The trial before Annas appears to have been a preliminary one. He questions Jesus. But Jesus reminds him of his public ministry and the many who had heard him teach. Why did he not ask them? Jesus refuses to repeat what the high priest ought to know about.

The impetuosity of the guard

The slap of the officer was an attempt to enforce authority. The lack of knowledge of what Jesus taught was an embarrassment to them. The action was an attempt at some demonstration of authority. Note Jesus' answer and the solution of sending him to Caiaphas.

> *Throughout the trial the principles of justice were not much in evidence. The climate of the trial was not conducive to that.*

JOHN 18:19, 20
The public ministry of Jesus

> *The preaching ministry of Jesus was widely known, at least in Galilee. His fame had spread far and wide as we know from the other gospels. Jesus appeals to the great number of witnesses as a reason for his not answering the high priest's question.*

Jesus wanted his ministry to be public

He was heard by multitudes. He taught in synagogues and in the open air. He wanted people to hear his teaching.

Jesus had nothing to hide

He claims that he had done nothing secretly. His ministry was not subversive. It was for the benefit of mankind.

Jesus challenges his accusers to produce evidence
The fact that everything was done in public shows the falseness of the charges brought against him.

When Jesus died he died unjustly. There were only trumped up charges brought against him. But the early Christians soon realised that he had in fact died on their behalf.

JOHN 18:15–18; 25–27
Denials by Peter

We cannot be sure who the other disciple was who was known to the high priest. But the story concentrates on Peter. It paints his portrait warts and all.

The circumstances
Peter was in the presence of the enemies of Jesus. It was a place of special temptation. After the injury inflicted on Malchus' ear, he would have been a marked man in the eyes of some.

The seriousness of the offence
He was the leading apostle. He had been with Jesus both in the upper room and in the garden. He had gone to see where Jesus had been taken. And then he denied him. To deny Jesus is a terrible sin.

The repetition worsened the offence
The maid at the door, the person at the fireside, the relative of Malchus all challenged him. Each time he denied. John spares Peter the mention of the swearing accompanying the last denial (Mk. 14:71). It is perhaps significant that he alone records the restoration (Jn. 21).

The awakening of his conscience
The cock crew. The sound of it must have rung in his ears
for a long time. He had been so sure it would not happen
when Jesus had predicted it. No wonder he broke down and
wept (as Mark tells us).

> *We must admire Peter's courage in going so
> far. But his failure must be a warning to all.
> No one is beyond the possibility of falling.*

JOHN 18:28–40
Jesus before Pilate

> *The Sanhedrin shows up in a bad light. They
> were anxious to act with an unseemly haste.*

An early visit to the praetorium
John omits the hearing before Caiaphas. We have seen his
strong bias against Jesus. His haste to send him to Pilate
early in the morning compacts his guilt. His hypocrisy is
seen from the fact that neither he nor those who took Jesus
would enter for fear of defilement. A ritual act is much
more important than the demand for the death of a righteous man.

An evasive answer about the accusation
The accusers' answer makes a mockery of the proceedings.
Did they really expect to get away without specifying the
charge? It is small wonder that Pilate rebukes them. But
John adds a significant comment that the Jews' request for
the death sentence fulfilled Jesus' own words – presumably
Jn. 12:32.

Pilate confronts Jesus
The question is political: 'Are you the king of the Jews?'
Jesus knew well that the chief priests had invented the
charge, and that it was not Pilate's own idea.
 The second question is: 'What have you done?' Jesus

points to a different kind of kingship which needs no support from violent means.

The third question is: 'So you are a king?' To this Jesus gives a guarded answer. He came for this purpose.

The fourth question is: 'What is truth?' It seems clear that Pilate asks it cynically. But he was addressing the one who said, 'I am the truth'. Pilate is clearly baffled.

The most striking thing about the trial of Jesus is that the judge comes under judgment rather than the prisoner. Pilate has ever since been remembered for his lack of justice.

JOHN 18:28
Defilement

There is irony in the fact that the religious accusers of Jesus are bent on ritual observance, even in face of a hasty attempt to pervert justice. This should warn us against wrong notions of defilement.

Different notions of defilement
Ceremonial defilement played an important part in Judaism. Ritual contacts were intended to be significant as a reminder that sin was to be avoided. But it was all too easy for ceremonial uncleanness to be avoided while spiritual uncleanness remained.

Ritual defilement is here rated as superior
These men had one evil intent – to get rid of Jesus. They have not considered the justice of their act, only its expediency. In view of such glaring spiritual guilt, why are they concerned about ritual uncleanness?

Defilement must always be a matter of the spirit
In that scene the only completely undefiled person was Jesus whom they were condemning. They could bring no

authentic accusation against him. The purity of Jesus stood as a condemnation of their empty ritualism.

> *Beware of the danger of relying on external ritual procedures which leave untouched the real uncleanness of the whole person.*

JOHN 18:36, 37
A kingship not from this world

> *When we think of kings, we think of earthly kings. But none of them, either despots or constitutional monarchs, are fitting analogies for the kingship of Jesus.*

A different kind of kingship

Jesus' kingdom is ruled on entirely different principles. It is essentially moral and spiritual. It makes greater demands on the subjects, for it expects no less than total commitment. And yet paradoxically it is not tyrannical for it works on the principle of love.

This kingship rejects the use of force

Few earthly kingdoms can escape the use of force. Pilate was a prime example of oppressive rule which relied on might at the expense of justice. It is significant that his misrule later caused his recall by the emperor.

This kingship finds expression in Jesus himself

He was born a king. He came not to exercise an over-lordship but to witness to truth. No wonder Pilate was baffled. Human history has never seen a king like this. Jesus' overriding aim was to bring light, not power or wealth, to his subjects.

> *Those who belong to the kingdom of God are members of two kingdoms, a heavenly and an*

earthly. Where allegiance clashes the heavenly
has the superior claim.

JOHN 18:38
What is truth?

The explanation that Jesus' kingdom was
concerned with truth baffles Pilate as it has
done many since. But Jesus has to show that
truth is more important than power.

Cynicism about truth

Pilate's question implies that there is no such thing as truth.
He does not appear to be asking with a serious desire to
know. With many truth is merely a matter of convenience.
If it gets in the way, they scoff at it.

Jesus' idea of truth

He unashamedly centres it on himself. Everyone attached
to truth hears his voice. This implies that anything out of
alignment with himself is not truth. He establishes himself
as the measure by which all claimants to truth must be
judged.

Pilate's question was not answered because
the enquiry was insincere. But when we ask in
faith we discover an open door of
understanding. The Christian has no doubt
that he knows the answer to Pilate's question.

JOHN 18:38–40
Barabbas

Pilate's perplexity is highlighted here. He admits there is no crime, but his solution is patently unjust.

No case to answer
This is a most extraordinary statement for Pilate to make. And yet he was uttering the truth. There was no crime in Jesus. He was without sin (cf. Heb. 7:26).

One man to release
Pilate's appeal to a Jewish custom shows his contempt, for he had little time for the Jews and their customs. He merely saw it as a way out. Did he expect the people to side with Jesus?

A substitute to suffer
A criminal is preferred to an innocent man. It was a clear case of substitution. Barabbas, in spite of his crimes, got off scot-free because Jesus died.

Justice was being blatantly denied. But the substitution of Jesus for Barabbas speaks volumes about the meaning of the cross for us.

JOHN 19:1–11
Pilate confronts Jesus

There is pathos in this scene. The governor represents all whose failure to appreciate the true nature of Jesus ends in bafflement and sheer irrationality.

The mockery
Pilate declares Jesus innocent and yet scourges him. The

soldiers crown him and yet with thorns. They hail him and yet with derisive slaps. And people are still mocking the king of kings.

The presentation
Pilate's unhappy appeal to them is rudely dismissed. His announcement, 'Behold the man!' roused their fury. And yet their cry has echoed through Christian history. They little thought how later generations would condemn them.

The accusation
'He has made himself Son of God.' The law to which the Jews appealed was presumably Lev. 24:16 which was the law of blasphemy. They regarded Jesus' claims as blasphemous simply because they did not believe them.

The defence
Pilate's fear arises from superstition. His further question to Jesus was greeted by silence. The agitated judge and the calm prisoner stand in vivid contrast. Pilate's appeal to power shows how important it is to him. Yet Jesus denies him any right in himself to any power.

Pilate the judge has stood before the bar of human judgment ever since. His weakness stands out in strong relief against the regal attitude of Jesus towards his accusers.

JOHN 19:2
The crown of thorns

The picture of Jesus wearing a crown of thorns has often been painted. Its symbolism is eloquent. Consider what it says to us today.

A symbol of man's inhumanity
It was intended to be cruel. No attention was paid to the intense suffering it imposed on the victim. It stands as a

rebuke to all who inflict torture on others to gain their own ends. It should be noted that the thorns contributed nothing to the justice of the occasion.

A symbol of humiliation

Was this the best that mankind could do to the only perfect man who ever lived? The thorns are symbolic of the whole mortal life of Jesus. Man should have crowned him with honour instead of shame. But cruelty still stalks the land against the representatives of good.

> *The crown of thorns mocks the royal role of Jesus. No purer head ever wore so cruel a crown. The time comes when that head will wear many diadems.*

JOHN 19:5
Ecce Homo!

Frequently profound statements are made by those who have no idea of their true significance. Here is one such statement.

An expression of Pilate's contempt

It is noticeable that Pilate did not say 'King' here. He regarded Jesus as no more than a man. This view has been shared by multitudes since who have failed to see that Jesus claims much more than that.

An expression of Jesus' humanity

The Christian church ever since has realised the importance of the humanity of Jesus. Some errors have arisen because the person of Jesus has been restricted to his humanity. But the first heresies denied his humanity altogether. *Ecce Homo* points to an essential truth.

An invitation for all to look

The words are an exhortation to see. Christians have responded, not in the way that Pilate meant, but in adoring wonder that God's son should endure such shame for their sakes. That vision of Jesus has inspired many who have since suffered for the cause of Christ.

If we would see perfect manhood, look at him. The call still goes out, 'Ecce Homo'.

JOHN 19:9
Where are you from?

The origin of Jesus has perplexed many. His accusers here have no doubts. He is a man of Nazareth. But Pilate detects some mystery. To fail to see more than human origin in Jesus is to fail to see Jesus.

Pilate's enigma

The question concerned Jesus. There was so much of which Pilate was ignorant. But Jesus is enigmatic to most people. Even some Christians cannot always answer the question. It needs faith and spiritual insight to grasp that Jesus came from above.

Jesus' response

He remained silent. Why? Because he wanted Pilate to know who was really in charge. The Roman governor or any other ruler exercised authority only by God's permission. Pilate felt more uneasy the more he thought about Jesus.

The early Christians soon discovered the answer. The divine origin of Jesus became an essential part of Christian belief and it still is.

JOHN 19:10, 11
Power and authority

Power corrupts. It is difficult for those who possess it to recognise that it carries great responsibility. Pilate's assertion and Jesus' correction are a salutary reminder of the true approach to power.

A false sense of power
Pilate thought he had authority to release or crucify Jesus. Any onlooker would have thought the same. He was after all the governor. He had been appointed by Caesar. But political power had nothing to do with the destiny of Jesus. Pilate was totally helpless in face of eternal realities, as many other rulers in human history have found.

A true sense of power
Jesus reminds Pilate that his so-called power is only delegated. It is not absolute. It can never be. The really powerful person in this drama is Jesus. He makes the arrogant and intensely cruel governor afraid. It is a tragedy that Pilate paid no attention to his conscience. He finds his prisoner disturbing.

There are right and wrong uses of power. We praise God for those rulers who have learned to restrain their power in the interests of the community. But most have abused power to their own undoing.

JOHN 19:12–16
Pilate gives in to the accusers

*If Pilate's behaviour before Jesus shows his
lack of understanding, he fared no better
when facing the accusers. But at least he
sought to release Jesus.*

A threat to the judge
'You are not Caesar's friend.' Pilate's position was precarious. Such a charge, if proved, could prove fatal.

A challenge to the accusers
'Here is your king!' Pilate uses the sarcasm he has already used in 18:39. He has no love for these Jews. He clearly did not believe Jesus was a king.

A demand by the accusers
'Crucify him.' Why did they demand a method of death they so hated when used by the Romans against masses of their own insurrectionists? John does not tell us. Their hatred of Jesus will stop at nothing.

A question from the judge
'Shall I crucify your king?' Pilate emphasises the word king for added sarcasm. The demand seemed to him ludicrous.

A retort from the accusers
'We have no king but Caesar.' Such a claim was even more ludicrous. As Jews they were supposed to acknowledge only God as king. Their words clearly show a lack of allegiance to him.

*The dialogue records the utter defeat of a
weak man. He surrenders Jesus to be
crucified.*

JOHN 19:17–25a
The crucifixion

John tells the story briefly and to the point. It is the climax of his story of Jesus. The pathos of it lives on to touch the hearts of all who read.

The way to crucifixion
Roman cruelty is seen in the demand of the condemned to carry their own instrument of punishment. John does not dwell on the fact that for part of the way another had to carry it for him.

The trio on crosses
Again John gives no details of the others with him, but we know that one railed at him and the other sought his help. Those on the other crosses symbolise alternative assessments of the one on the middle cross, one for the other against.

The inscription on Jesus' cross
In spite of his surrender Pilate will not pander to the Jewish objections to the 'king' title. It added to their chagrin that he had it displayed in three languages.

The casting of lots below the cross
It was the normal procedure for the soldiers on duty to share the clothing. The casting of lots decided the owner. But John sees a fulfilment of Ps. 22:18. The high priest's robe should not be torn (Ex. 28:32).

As Jesus died we see the obstinacy of Pilate, the quibbling of the religious rulers and the avarice of the soldiers. What is our attitude to be?

JOHN 19:23, 24
Dividing the garments

*The soldiers casting lots beneath the dying
Jesus draws attention to another sordid aspect
of the whole proceedings.*

An illustration of human baseness
The stripping of Jesus added to the indignity which was
cruelly imposed upon him. The soldiers were devoid of all
sensitivity. Their avarice in wanting a share of the spoils
stands out in bleak contrast to the self-giving spirit of Jesus.

An insight into Jesus' manner of life
The cloak was a simple peasant's robe. Jesus wore no
finery. His life style was of the simplest kind. He identified
with the lowliest of his people.

A fulfilment of Scripture
John sees scripture as pointing to Christ. This is amply
illustrated elsewhere in the New Testament. The soldiers
were oblivious of the fact that they were fulfilling an ancient
prediction. But John sees God's hand even in the casting of
lots.

*Does it ever concern us that we might be
wanting to gain anything from him who gave
everything for us?*

JOHN 19:25b–27
John and the women at the cross

*Into the grim account of crucifixion, John
interjects an incident which focuses on a
more humane side.*

The women's concern for Jesus

The disciples, except for John, had all fled. Only the
women stayed. Why did they stay? Would not the dreadful
scene have deeply offended their sensitivities? It was love
that did it. The four women have ever since shamed the
cowardice of the disciples. They must have brought great
comfort to Jesus as he looked down on them.

Jesus' concern for his mother

He knew better than anyone else what she was suffering to
see him suffer. He knew she needed support. Who better to
do this than the beloved disciple? Note the conciseness of
the arrangement. 'Behold your son . . . Behold your
mother!'

*Did John take her away immediately? Or did
they stay to the end? His action on behalf of
Jesus serves as a pattern of compassion for all
time.*

JOHN 19:28–30
The cry of triumph

*In this brief section we have two sayings from
the cross. They speak of what was in Jesus'
mind at the point of death.*

The cry of thirst

(a) It shows Jesus shared our human nature. Thirst is

agonising, and he had probably had no drink since leaving the upper room.

(b) It shows the acuteness of his suffering. Crucifixion was the worst torture that man could devise, but this was made worse through denial of drink. How tragic that the Lord of creation was so treated!

(c) It shows what could be done to minister to him. Some had thought enough about the suffering to provide vinegar to moisten the parched lips. This was necessary if the cry immediately after was to be heard.

The cry of fulfilment

The words 'It is finished' are one word in the Aramaic. It was not a word of defeat but of victory. It means accomplished. The task the Father had given was now done. It marked the close of his earthly life and the accomplishing of redemption. He was ready to give up his spirit.

The concluding cry which John records still rings out for mankind to hear. The cross is no place of disillusionment. It is the place of the finished work of Christ.

JOHN 19:31–37
The piercing

After Jesus' death we find different approaches to his body. The differences are due to the different backgrounds from which it was viewed.

The Jews' ritual concern

It was the approach of the sabbath which caused the anxiety. Again there is incongruity when callous cruelty and ritual concern go hand in hand.

211

Pilate's concession

John does not mention any dialogue between the Jews and Pilate. The hard-hearted judge raises no objection to the soldiers hastening the deaths. We may be sure it was not out of regard for Jewish scruples.

The soldiers' piercing

Since Jesus was already dead, the leg-breaking was unnecessary. But so was the piercing. It seems to have been an impulsive act of further brutality. But John's comment on the act has outlived the act itself.

The evangelist's testimony

The personal witness verifies the reality. John saw the blood and water pour out. He probably regarded it as symbolic of the life which came from Jesus' death. He moreover remembered two more scriptures which were fulfilled by the soldier's action.

None of the accounts of the death of Jesus suggest that the events happened by accident. In the fulfilment of scripture the Christians saw evidence that God was at work.

JOHN 19:38–42
The embalming of the body

The burial of the body of Jesus has always been an important part of Christian belief (cf. 1 Cor. 15:4). It may be regarded as a necessary prelude to the resurrection.

Two notable friends of Jesus

The crucifixion had emboldened two secret followers. Both were influential men. Joseph was wealthy; Nicodemus was a respected Jewish leader. It was Joseph who asked Pilate for the body.

The last act of devotion to Jesus
Both men embalm the body with spices. Their act of love has engraved their names in the history of the event. Note the considerable cost of their act of love.

The provision of a tomb for Jesus
According to Mt. 27:60 the tomb belonged to Joseph but he readily made it available to take the body of Jesus. It was to be the scene of the triumph of the resurrection. But we remember that Jesus lay in a borrowed tomb.

It takes a crisis to spur some people into open allegiance to Jesus. Are we inhibited through fear from making known that we are followers of Jesus?

JOHN 20:1–10
The empty tomb

The emptiness of the tomb does not in itself prove the resurrection but it contributes a strong testimony to it.

A woman discovers the empty tomb
It says much for Mary's devotion that she goes while it is still dark. But she could see the stone was rolled away. Her consequent deduction was wrong, but her keenness is commendable.

Peter and John enter the empty tomb
John arrives before Peter and notes the folded clothes. Peter rushes in to see for himself and John follows. John notes down that he believed. He does not tell us what he believed. Had it at this stage dawned on him that Jesus must rise? As yet he had not seen him.

*That the tomb was empty must be regarded as
a fact of history. Those theories which explain
it by natural means are fraught with more
problems than that which affirms that God had
raised Jesus from the dead.*

JOHN 20:9
The necessity for the resurrection

*The early Christian belief in the resurrection
did not arise out of a belief that scripture must
be fulfilled. The sequence was the other way
round.*

The conviction that Jesus had risen came first
As they gazed at the empty tomb the seeds of faith began. It
needed to be reinforced by the appearances and still later
by the realisation that scripture had predicted it.

The recognition of scriptural prediction came later
But what scripture had predicted the necessity of the
resurrection? Some have suggested Isa. 53:10–12 or Ps.
16:10. Christians were firmly convinced that the Old Testament pointed to the resurrection of Christ. It was as much
part of his destiny as his death. Note the word 'must' in this
context.

*The work of redemption would have been
incomplete without a rising from the dead.*

JOHN 20:11–18
Mary Magdalene

She is one of the most fascinating people who appear on the gospel pages. She is still a challenge to us in the wholeheartedness of her devotion.

Her devotion to Jesus
Not only was she the first at the tomb: she stayed there and kept watching. Her tears were eloquent of her love.

Her vision of angels
She had to look into the tomb to see them. She gives as the reason for her weeping that some people (unspecified) have taken her Lord away. Her mind was on the body of Jesus – she had no understanding as yet of the resurrection.

Her meeting with Jesus
Through tearful eyes she mistakes him for the gardener. The 'they' of verse 13 has become 'you' in verse 15. But no one had taken him away. The voice was no gardener's voice. It was unmistakably the voice of Jesus.

Her touching of Jesus
We are not told where she held on. But Jesus stops it. Touch belongs to physical not spiritual existence. She had to learn a different kind of relationship.

Her commission from Jesus
She had the honoured task of announcing to the disciples that Jesus was ascending to the Father. He was not dead, but alive.

Mary loved much because she owed so much to Jesus. But her ardour needed correcting because it was based on wrong ideas. How far is she a pattern for modern believers in her devotion to Jesus?

JOHN 20:11–18
Sorrow turned to joy

*Jesus had promised such a spiritual alchemy
(Jn. 16:20). Mary was the first to experience it.*

The cause of Mary's sorrow
It was wrongly based, for she sorrowed over a dead Christ
and he was no longer dead. She had her facts wrong. Her
tears were quite unnecessary.

The reason for Mary's joy
She heard a familiar voice calling her name. She received
no answer to her question. It wasn't needed. She would
know that voice anywhere. The presence of Jesus made all
the difference.

The spreading of Mary's joy
She was not to keep the joy to herself. Where transformation has taken place others should know about it: 'I have
seen the Lord.' That was the unspeakable joy which she
spread.

*There is no sorrow that Jesus cannot turn into
joy. There is no joy like the joy of knowing the
risen Lord.*

JOHN 20:15
Weeping for the wrong reason

John has three references to weeping. He records how Jesus wept (11:35). He notes the prediction of Jesus that the disciples would weep (16:20). And now describes the weeping of Mary.

Weeping is not seen as a sign of weakness

If Jesus wept there is no reason why Mary should not weep. It is recognised that tears are therapeutic at times of bereavement. Mary's tears over a dead Christ are understandable and commendable.

Weeping over a dead Christ when he is alive is misplaced

Human emotion does not always size up a situation objectively. It is a lesson for every situation where tears begin to flow. First reflect on whether they are justified.

Weeping is out of keeping when the risen Christ appears

Note the repeated question, 'Woman, why are you weeping?' In face of the glorious fact that Jesus has conquered death, weeping is inappropriate. Indeed he has inaugurated an era which will end in the banishment of all tears (Cf. Rev. 21:4).

It is easy to weep for the wrong reason. But we need to examine our attitudes and emotions. Are our tears really justified?

JOHN 20:19–23
The appearance to the disciples

*Here was the first appearance to the disciples
as a group. They were sharing their experience
of desolation over Jesus' death when
unexpectedly he appears.*

Jesus stands in their midst
John does not tell us where they met, but the doors were closed. They were still gripped with fear. Their world had fallen apart, but they at least met together. When the risen Lord shows them his hands, they could be in no doubt about whose hands they were.

Jesus gives them peace
He does this twice. It was clearly of great importance. Their minds just then were anything but peaceful.

Jesus commissions them
It is simple but profound. 'As the Father sent me' sums up his earthly mission. 'Even so send I you' sums up the church's mission. The parallel is significant and awesome.

Jesus bestows on them the Spirit
The breathing on them ties up with the idea of the Spirit as wind. Did they receive the Spirit at once? Some think they did. Others that this foreshadowed Pentecost. The main thought is that Jesus is the giver. The forgiving and retaining of sins must also be a God-given gift.

*Their first encounter with the risen Lord
results in two wonderful gifts. Since peace is
one of the fruits of the Spirit, the two are
inseparable.*

JOHN 20:20
Gladness over the risen Lord

Gladness came to the disciples on the first Easter day. The fact that Jesus is alive has ever since been a source of the greatest joy to believers.

They were glad when they saw the wound prints
Those wound prints conclusively identified Jesus. The disciples had great sorrow over the death of Jesus. They were afraid for the future. But now that he was alive everything was transformed. The very wound prints became a testimony to his self-sacrifice for their sake.

They were glad when they heard his voice
It was the same voice. They had heard that word of peace before (14:27). Jesus knew how much they needed it. It was like soothing ointment to their troubled spirits. Sorrow was being turned to joy before their eyes.

They were glad when they understood his mission
Jesus told them he was sending them as the Father had sent him. As yet they had no idea what this would involve. But the more they reflected on the life of Jesus as a life lived for the Father, the more they must have understood.

The reality of the risen Christ is as indisputable for us. For we too can have the great joy of hearing his comforting voice of peace and his commissioning us for God's work.

JOHN 20:21
The risen Lord's commission

The work of the Christian church does not originate in the decision of a committee. It is Christ saying to his followers 'I send you'.

The Father's commission to the Son
Consider the motive for the sending. Jn. 3:16 gives the reason. The plan of redemption was a plan of love. It was carried out by the Son in obedience to the Father.

The Son's commission to the disciples
What was expected of them? Certainly an identification with the mission of Christ. This would involve a similar compassion and love for others. It would also involve self-sacrifice.

The comparison between them
Many times in this gospel comparisons are made between God's action and ours. His becomes the pattern for ours. Ours must show dependency on the same source of power. Ours must be seen as a continuation of God's mission in Christ. It is a highly challenging comparison.

It should be remembered that the commission was dependent on the gift of the Holy Spirit. It would otherwise be impossible.

JOHN 20:24–29
Thomas meets the risen Lord

*Thomas is the representative of all doubters.
Many have thanked God that this account of
his scepticism and its solution was included in
this gospel. His is a position with which it is
easy to identify.*

Thomas the absentee
We would like to know why he was absent on Easter day.
Had he given up through discouragement? Had he been
persuaded by someone since to rejoin the others? His
reluctance to meet with the others on Easter day suggests
that his doubts had already taken strong root.

Thomas the sceptic
The disciples told him of their encounter with Jesus. They
must have described the wound prints. But Thomas wants
more definite proof. Did he really want to handle the
wounds? He clearly never imagined it was possible, so
profound was his scepticism.

Thomas the believer
Eight days later he is with the rest. He has at least joined
them. When Jesus appears it is as if no one else mattered
but Thomas. How tenderly he dealt with the sceptic! He too
receives the word of peace. But how embarrassing for
Thomas is the invitation to put the finger in the hand wound
and the hand in the side wound in the precise terms of
Thomas' demand. It was enough – faith displaced his
scepticism.

Thomas the theologian
Now that all doubt has gone, Thomas expresses a profound
truth. 'My Lord and my God' is a more profound view of
Jesus than that of any of the others. Doubt seems to have
paved the way for greater understanding. It did the same
with the apostle Paul and has done the same for many
others since.

The doubts were honest enough. But when doubt collapsed, thoroughgoing conviction at once took its place. Never regard doubt as final. It can often lead to deeper assurance. Jesus notes the added blessedness of believing without sight.

JOHN 20:28
From doubt to faith

Listen to a man confessing the deity of Christ. It was John's purpose that his readers should come to a high view of Jesus. Here the confession is on the lips of the doubter Thomas.

It showed an understanding of the character of Jesus
To call Jesus God raises all kind of problems for many theologians. But Thomas plunges in to grasp the possibility that the one he had lived with was none other than God. His confession goes beyond Peter's insight at Caesarea Philippi. It challenges the lesser views of Jesus current in some quarters today.

It showed a personal relationship with Jesus
Thomas was no abstract theologian. The double use of the word 'my' in his statement points to a meaningful relationship. It was bold to use the possessive in this way, but it forms a pattern for believers still. We may boldly appropriate Jesus as Lord and God as Thomas did.

Deep thinkers have never exhausted the significance of these words. They still stand as a challenge to the modern church. We dare not dispense with them simply because we cannot fathom them.

JOHN 20:29
The blessedness of faith

*To many faith and sight are inseparable. The
saying that seeing is believing sums up an
attitude of scepticism as if believing without
seeing is out of the question. But Jesus puts a
different complexion on the matter.*

All cannot see, but all can believe
The disciples were privileged to see Jesus in the flesh. But
subsequent generations cannot set eyes on him. Yet the
greater blessedness is for those who believe without seeing.

All need not see, but all need to believe
This is the age of the Spirit in which we see Jesus in a
different way. Every Christian believes because his eyes
have been opened to see him (cf. 2 Cor. 4:5, 6).

All who see do not necessarily believe
Many saw Jesus in the flesh and did not believe. Some
mocked, some ignored, some crucified. People may today
see Jesus through the lives of others, but the challenge to
personal faith still remains.

All who believe without seeing have a special blessing
Jesus is virtually saying that believing is the most important
exercise of all, even for those who were with him in the
flesh.

*In a spiritual sense seeing is believing for those
who are ready to respond to the revelation of
God. But it is seeing in a new way.*

JOHN 20:30, 31
John states his purpose

The writer selects his material
He knows of many other events and words. He presumably
knows about the other gospels. But as a master craftsman
he knows he must be selective. He would have been
restricted for space whether he had used a scroll or a codex.
He was given special wisdom to know what to leave out.

The writer states his purpose
We must be thankful that John takes the trouble to tell us
why he writes. Had he not done so many theories would
have been concocted to explain it. As it is theories still
abound, but all must take account of this statement.

The writer admits a theological aim
He wants his readers to believe. He has an unashamedly
evangelistic purpose. He focuses not on Jesus' earthly life,
but on faith in Jesus' person – Christ and Son of God. His
book was designed to lead to such a view of Jesus. Anyone
with such faith would receive life in Jesus' name. None of
the other evangelists express their purpose so plainly.

*Throughout Christian history people have
been reading John's gospel and believing in
Jesus. But it must be admitted that some read
it and never find life. What does this gospel
mean to us?*

JOHN 21:1–8
Fishing in Galilee

*Of all the appearances this is singular in being
set in a familiar place amid familiar activity.*

The scene
Jesus goes back to Galilee. It was there he first called his
disciples. The fishing scene echoes a similar setting. Was
this to remind them of their calling?

The disciples
Five are named and two are left unnamed. The first three
named are all mentioned earlier in the gospel. John has a
special interest in showing they again met with Jesus. These
were to form the witnesses to Peter's restoration.

The activity
At Peter's suggestion they resumed their old occupation.
Had they lost their touch? They caught nothing until Jesus
told them where to fish. It speaks highly for them that they
obeyed the voice. At what point did they know it was the
voice of Jesus?

The response
John was first to recognise. Peter hurried to meet Jesus.
The rest coped with the large catch of fish. The different
responses illustrate the different reactions to the revelation
of the risen Christ.

*The disciples were showing diligence in their
fishing. It is often in the midst of daily work
that God comes to us rather than in times of
special meditation.*

JOHN 21:9–14
Barbecue on the beach

*This incident is charming because it is so
natural. It teaches us something about the
approach of Jesus to human needs.*

The charcoal fire
Where had it come from? Jesus must have provided it. A
cooked breakfast after a night of frustrating fruitlessness
was just what they needed. But did that charcoal fire
remind Peter of his denial? – cf. 18:18.

The call for fish
Jesus made no provision for this except by giving advice to
the disciples. They did not need the 153 fishes they caught.
Why did they count them? The marvel was the unbroken
net.

The distribution of bread and fish
Did they remember when they similarly handed out bread
and fish to the multitudes? The miracle was different but no
less impressive. Why were they afraid to ask who he was?
The fact is they knew. True faith does not have to ask.

*The alfresco breakfast was preparatory for an
important occasion: the restitution of Peter.
We may reflect on what his thoughts may have
been as he watched Jesus cook the meal?*

JOHN 21:15–17
The restoration of Peter

Jesus had already appeared to Peter. But as yet he had not been restored in front of other witnesses. This is the main purpose of this encounter.

The threefold question
The threefold nature of it was to give Peter an opportunity to rectify his threefold denial. Its emphasis on love was in line with Jesus' farewell teaching. Significantly Jesus does not ask, 'Do you believe in me?' Note the threefold address to 'Simon son of John' instead of his usual name 'Peter'.

The first answer and Jesus' reply
Do the words 'more than these' mean more than the other disciples loved? Or is it comparing Peter's love for Jesus with his love for the others, or even his love for fishing? The first is most probable. He had boasted more. He had denied more. Did he love more? Peter affirms his love without making any comparisons. The first reply is 'Feed my lambs'.

The second answer and Jesus' reply
The second question drops the comparison and is therefore more straightforward. Peter's answer is nevertheless exactly the same. The second reply, 'Tend my sheep', is basically the same as the first.

The third answer and Jesus' reply
The third approach grieved Peter. It must have reminded him of his third denial. The answer was fuller – you know everything. The reply, 'Feed my sheep', although different in wording, is nevertheless essentially the same as the previous exhortations.

In the subsequent work of Peter he must often have thought about the commission he had received (cf. 1 Pet. 5:2–4). The task of tending

the flock is not yet finished. Peter's
commission is the church's commission.

JOHN 21:15–17
The pastoral office

*The simple account of Peter's restoration
contains some valuable lessons for those
engaged in pastoral work.*

Its basis is love for Jesus
Why so much emphasis on love? Jesus is stressing the importance of personal commitment to himself. No effective work is possible without this.

Its requirement is love for others
Those devoted to Jesus Christ will have something of his concern for others. A shepherd must love his sheep. The quality of his care for them will be affected by his love for them.

Its involvement is the nourishment of the flock
John uses two different words in recording Jesus' commission. One is the general word for shepherding; the other is the more intimate word for tending. But both are concerned with the welfare of the flock. The feeding process is vital for the flock.

*The shepherd imagery has always been
suggestive for the pastoral office. All analogies
have their weaknesses and people are very
different from sheep. But the care side is of
importance to both.*

JOHN 21:18–23
Predictions about the future

*Jesus looks ahead to events in the lives of two
of his followers. They are very different in
their temperament and in their destinies.*

Peter's future
After receiving reassurances from Jesus, Peter now hears
something of his destiny. He will not have any control over
it. It will contrast dramatically with his earliest years. The
binding is generally thought to refer to some form of violent
death. Tradition has it that he was crucified.

John's future
Peter's curiosity is aroused. But Jesus does not respond to
mere curiosity. His answer to Peter's question appears
harsh. It was tantamount to saying 'Mind your own business'. But the form of words gave rise to rumour. In fact
Jesus says of John only that his future will be determined by
Jesus' will, and he refuses to divulge what that will is.

*No one knows what the future holds. It is
sufficient to know that all will work out
according to a higher will. Our destiny is not
left to chance.*

JOHN 21:19
God glorified in death

*John adds a note of explanation here which is
startling. It accepts the premise that a man's
death can glorify God.*

Peter's life was intended to glorify God
The commission just received was not a sinecure to boost
Peter's ego. The shepherd task, properly carried out,

would bring glory to God as the rest of the New Testament shows.

Peter's death was equally intended to glorify God

The blood of the martyrs has been the seed of the church. Frequently the killing of God's servants has had more impact on survivors than their lives. This pattern is amply illustrated in the history of the church.

Since our lives are in God's hands the manner of death is equally in his hands. Peter's immediate task was not to be concerned about destiny, but about following Jesus.

JOHN 21:21, 22
Curiosity rebuked

We all like to know. 'What about this or that?' is often on our lips. But there are dangers.

The reasons for curiosity

In itself curiosity is good. Many inventions are the result of probing for knowledge. But in Peter's case it was not good because it was personal. We should take an interest in others without falling into the trap of wanting to compare ourselves with them.

The harmfulness of curiosity

Having heard about his own destiny Peter pries into the destiny of John. It is natural but harmful to concern ourselves with other people's affairs because it can lead to damaging gossip.

The rebuke of curiosity

The rebuke is stated in obscure terms. 'What is that to you?' implies the question ought to be dropped. The condition is expressed in an extreme form – suppose it is Jesus' will that

230

John should live until the second coming? We can understand how a wrong rumour got around.

We should use our curiosity in the right way
but beware of using it for idle gossip.

JOHN 21:24, 25
The conclusion to the Gospel

The last two verses consist of two postscripts,
one by the writer and the other by those who
could vouch for what he had done.

The writer's testimony
The writer is claiming to have been a witness of what he has
written. This clearly adds considerable weight to his witness. He is virtually telling us he did not make it up.

The supporting testimony of others
'We know that his testimony is true' means that there were
others involved in the publication of the gospel. When
witness is supported it is strengthened, and the comment
here shows the concern of the early church about the
authenticity of its accepted writings.

The omissions
There is so much else that could be told. But the world
would not be able to contain the books that would need to
be written. In this hyperbolical way we are left with the
impression of the pricelessness of those records we have in
our possession.

So ends this profound book about Jesus. It
still fascinates those who read it.

Further Hodder Christian Paperbacks to inform, entertain and deepen your faith.

THE SOLDIER'S ARMOURY

The Salvation Army

Written by Major Kenneth Lawson, these popular Bible reading notes are read daily by thousands of Christians of all denominations. An aid to the regular study of the whole Bible, *The Soldier's Armoury* offers fresh ideas, depth of insight and material for reflection and prayer.

'Demonstrates that daily Bible reading can actually be an exciting exercise . . . Warmly recommended.' *Baptist Times*

DOES JESUS CARE?

R. T. Kendall

'Do you know the feeling of being completely let down by the one you thought was the only person that could help you? But what if that last resort was Jesus? Surely he cares.'

Martha and Mary had their faith in Jesus shaken to its very core when he didn't respond to their plea to help Lazarus. He died. It must have seemed a devastating rejection at the time, and so it is for many Christians whose expectation of Jesus seems to lead only to disappointment. Perhaps a loved one dies despite earnest prayer, a job falls through, or plans collapse even after prayerful preparation. Are we to believe that Jesus·cares when he hears the cry of his people and does nothing?

'Yes,' affirms R. T. Kendall. 'This book will show not only that he cares but that he cares more deeply and painstakingly than you or I can begin to imagine.'

Dr R. T. KENDALL is minister of Westminster Chapel, and author of *Tithing* and *Once Saved, Always Saved*.

THE INSTITUTES OF CHRISTIAN RELIGION

John Calvin

An abridged popular edition edited by Tony Lane and Hilary Osborne

John Calvin's monumental *Institutes* has greatly influenced each generation since its writing in the middle of the sixteenth century. It is the most systematic presentation of the faith of the Reformation, and in its four original volumes covers the full breadth of biblically based theology.

In this edition, Tony Lane and Hilary Osborne have selected and sometimes abridged the most important texts in order to make Calvin more accessible to today's reader. The essential texts are here and cover amongst other topics, the absolute sovereignty of God, the centrality of the Bible in all matters of belief, behaviour and church government and man's inability to obtain salvation apart from God's free grace.

John Calvin (1509–1564). French protestant theologian and reformer, is especially known for his work in Geneva and his exposition of the doctrines of justification by faith and predestination.

EXPLORING GOD'S WORD

Bible Guide to Ephesians, Philippians and Colossians

Donald Guthrie

This informative *Bible Guide* covers three central New Testament books: Ephesians, Philippians and Colossians. The shape and detail of each is broken down into clear outlines to provide an illuminating explanation of the texts. Drawing on his intimate knowledge of the New Testament, and his skill in Bible teaching, Dr Guthrie shows how the Bible can and should bear fruit in the life of every Christian.

Ideal for groups, and a valuable resource for all who study the Bible, this first *Bible Guide* in the *Exploring God's Word* series will assist many to learn afresh from the living words of Scripture.